The Dirt Road

Janete Teixeira-Parente

ISBN 979-8-88751-142-9 (paperback)
ISBN 979-8-89526-801-8 (hardcover)
ISBN 979-8-88751-144-3 (digital)

Copyright © 2024 by Janete Teixeira-Parente

All rights reserved. No part of this publication may be reproduced, distributed, or transmitted in any form or by any means, including photocopying, recording, or other electronic or mechanical methods without the prior written permission of the publisher. For permission requests, solicit the publisher via the address below.

Christian Faith Publishing
832 Park Avenue
Meadville, PA 16335
www.christianfaithpublishing.com

Printed in the United States of America

To my nephews:
Emerson, Rafael, Joao Miguel, Nathan, and Benicio.
My nieces:
Ana, Lorena, and Iara
And to future generations
I love you unconditionally

Foreword

Written by Lauren Hammer

Janete and I met in September 2019 for what I thought would be a typical introductory networking meeting. It was anything but that. We skipped over the usual exchange of details about our businesses—Janete's medical billing company and my coaching and psychotherapy practices—and got right down to what I most enjoy—getting to know each other. Two hours later, I walked out of the coffee shop where I had laughed and cried, feeling in awe of the the woman I now call a friend.

Janete spoke proudly about growing up in Brazil with her family in a two-bedroom house at the end of a dirt road. She vividly recalled sharing one of the rooms with her siblings; they slept on corn husk mattresses made by her mother. Janete is the third of eleven children, the youngest nineteen years her junior. Sadly, her parents' first born only lived a few months, and their seventh died at the age of twenty-seven in an accident. Meals were prepared on their wood-burning stove, without running water or electricity. Janete relied upon the light from a kerosene lamp to do her homework, which she didn't begin until after a full day of school and working on the family farm.

In my twenty-five-plus-year career of working with clients facing various personal and professional challenges, I have never heard of a life story like Janete's. She's the only person I know who worked as a nanny, first-grade teacher, and bank teller during high school, let alone saved enough money to build her parents a four-bedroom house with running water and electricity. Yes, she did that!

Janete doesn't see herself as remarkable, but I do. Her humble and driven nature matches her quiet determination and drive. She's unknowingly inspirational and impressive. She's achieved so much in life, and all you know thus far is what she accomplished before attending college. There's so much more. You'll see.

I eagerly told my family about Janete that night over dinner. I shared stories about her experiences (poverty) and what she had (many jobs) and didn't have (water or electricity). My kids were fourteen and sixteen at the time, and there's no doubt that they noticed the juxtaposition of their lives to Janete's when she was their age. I hope they realize they can achieve their goals, provided they have the drive, focus, and interest to work hard.

Though we were born only one year apart, Janete and I grew up in different worlds. I grew up in suburban New Jersey, unknowingly taking for granted all the modern comforts Janete lacked. And when I got my first job at fourteen, I never considered sharing my $3.35 hourly pay with my parents.

Life is not a competition of who has it more challenging; we all have difficulties and we all have opportunities to work on our response to them. Believe me, it was heartbreaking to be twenty-three and watch my mother die, and I can't imagine being my husband at seventeen when police officers told him that his father had died by suicide. I also can't imagine facing all that Janete experienced as a child. I don't know how she had the wherewithal to realize at such a young age that she wanted more for herself and her family, and that she could make that happen.

When I asked Janete about her goal for writing The Dirt Road, her eyes welled up with tears, and she talked about wanting to inspire her four nephews and three nieces. She wants them to read her book and believe they, too, can achieve anything they want if they're willing to work hard. She wants to encourage them to go out into the world with the determination to conquer it. To know that they have choices in life and decisions to make. To believe that they will be okay regardless of what happens in their lives. And to always know that they are a source of light in her life and that she hopes to be one in theirs, too.

    My respect for Janete is immeasurable; the obstacles she has faced and her achievements are remarkable. Being asked to write this Foreword was an honor and a welcomed surprise—not only because I have yet to read The Dirt Road but because I practically begged Janete to write it. I'm so happy she agreed to put pen to paper and am thrilled it will be published for all to read. Janete's words will undoubtedly inspire you to do whatever it takes to ensure that you, like her, are always going down your very own dirt road.

Author's note

I am pleased to have the opportunity to share my experiences and insights through this book. "The Dirt Road" is a reflection of my journey, filled with challenges and triumphs. My hope is that this book inspires my nephews and nieces, as well as readers, to believe in their own capabilities and to persevere in the face of adversity. I invite you to join me in exploring the themes of resilience, determination, and the power of faith.

I have changed names throughout the story to preserve the characters' identities. In some harmless stories from my childhood, I omitted the characters' last names to protect their privacy.

Thank you for embarking on this journey with me.

Vienna

May 2019

Vienna, Austria's capital, lies in the country's east on the Danube River, its artistic and intellectual legacy shaped by world-famous residents, including Mozart, Beethoven, and Sigmund Freud. The city is known for its imperial palaces, including Schönbrunn, the Habsburgs' summer residence.

On my tenth wedding anniversary, I found myself in the splendid city of Vienna, a place I had only encountered through captivating photographs and history books. Standing there, I was utterly captivated by its exquisite elegance, rich history, and breathtaking architecture.

I was sitting by my hotel window overlooking the beautiful St. Stephen's Cathedral and admiring the people walking back and forth and the cafés with their outdoor dining. This reminded me of Curitiba, the beautiful capital of my home state in Brazil, with the famous Rua das Flores. For a moment, the similarity of the two cities caused me to feel homesick. Even the weather seemed the same—rain, sun, and cold, almost all the seasons on the same day.

The breathtaking beauty of Vienna brought back memories of my humble beginnings in Campina do Diamante, a rural area later renamed Agua Clara. It was a place where the only sound was the song of birds perched on the branches of the massive trees that bordered the many miles of dusty dirt road. Standing there, I reflected on my journey from farm girl to where I am today. I wondered if my nieces and nephews would ever get to hear about the experiences that shaped me. Would they see beyond the aunt who intermittently brings gifts from far away places, unknown to them? I pondered whether there would ever be a moment when I could sit down with them and share my life story.

As I continued to explore the enchanting city of Vienna, the desire to impart my story and life lessons to my beloved nephews and nieces grew stronger. I wished to convey to them the importance of understanding that challenges and setbacks are an integral part of the human experience and that every obstacle presents an opportunity for learning and personal growth. I hoped to instill a resilient attitude towards life's trials, urging them to confront challenges head-on and derive valuable lessons from each experience. In this metaphorical "school of life," I wanted them to realize that the most demanding courses often yield the most profound insights and that both success and occasional failure are natural aspects of the learning process.

I desired for them to embrace the beauty of perseverance, never to shy away from trying again, and to cultivate a firm determination.

I wanted them to understand the intrinsic worth of hard work, instill a deep sense of responsibility and work ethic, and emphasize that true greatness is achieved through dedication and untiring effort.

Also, I wanted to inspire them to find their passion and pursue it.

Adapt to the challenges coming along the way, and life will take them places.

Never hesitate to dream big because great things will not come from their comfort zone.

Don't fear the unknown. Be a risk taker and a challenger. It's better to try than to regret.

If you are frightened of losing, you have already lost.

Be kind to those around you, and never compare yourself to anyone because the scar of your failures and the medals of your accomplishments will tell your unique story.

Remember that doing the right thing is always right, especially when no one is watching.

Never forget where you came from, your family, friends, and God.

As my husband and I embarked on our journey to celebrate our tenth wedding anniversary, thoughts of my nephews and nieces accompanied us, imagining the day when they, too, could explore the world and discover its wonders.

Childhood

When I was five years old, in 1976, I held my mother's hand and walked five hundred meters from our house to enroll in first grade. My sister, Diolete, was seven then, and neither of us had a birth certificate. When Diolete was born, my dad couldn't afford the fee for her birth certificate. Over time, the outstanding fees grew. Then I was born, and the financial burden on my father increased even more. Because we lived in a small rural community where everyone knew each other, my mother had no trouble enrolling her second child in school without any documentation.

The school near our farm didn't have a preschool program, so kids would start attending school at the age of six in first grade. I had spent the previous year crying after my sister Diolete as she set out for school each morning. I was eager to join her in the learning experience. Every day, as I awaited her return from school, I hoped she would share the new things she had learned with me, but she never did. Instead of holding a grudge, I kept turning to my mom, repeatedly pleading to start going to school and learning. My mom finally gave in and enrolled me in school at the age of five. Fortunately, the school accepted me a year earlier than most students.

After what seemed like an eternity, the day arrived when I found myself sitting in the same classroom with my sister. The books at our school, a prized possessions, captivated by me, each filled with many vibrant and astonishing images I had never encountered. The intricate pictures of ducks gracefully adorning the pages and the charming illustrations of houses inspired amazement and wonder within me.

THE DIRT ROAD

Our school was a solitary structure, an old building with shattered windows that allowed the biting winter winds to seep in. Southern Brazil can be exceptionally cold during winter, especially for a young child like myself. I navigated the harsh cold in nothing but flip-flops. I had no hat, no warm coat. I shivered and my hands grew numb as I clutched the plastic grocery bag that held my notebook and pencil.

As I stepped into the warmth of the classroom, I flexed and exercised my fingers, allowing the blood to flow back into them before I opened my notebook. The wooden desks, spoke of a past era, dating back to the time of my father's youth, and they were slightly worn from years of abuse, having been engraved with scribbles of disinterested students years earlier. I vividly remember trying to decipher what those scribbles meant; some were beautiful drawings, but I could never understand.

In a small classroom designed to accommodate first to fourth-graders, a commanding teacher led the students with authority. Her robust and professional voice resonated throughout the room, ensuring that all the students could grasp her teachings as she skillfully managed the wide range of grades in the classroom. As a curious kid, I often observed my classmates' books and notebooks, and the teacher frequently had to gently remind me to finish my work before examining what my friends were doing.

All of my classmates, without exception, conducted themselves with extraordinary respect toward one another, creating a conducive environment for effective learning under the guidance of our teacher, who had also been my father's teacher many years ago. She was a delightful woman, affectionately referred to by her nickname, Dona Mana, with profound respect. In Brazil, it is customary to use the word "Dona" before a name or nickname to formally and respectfully address women, a tradition that perseveres.

I feel immensely fortunate to have been under the guidance of Dona Mana, my first and second-grade teacher, and her daughter, Tera, who taught me during my third and fourth-grade years. Their mentorship went beyond the classroom, nurturing the love for learning and the thirst for knowledge that continues to shape my life.

Dona Mana and Tera provided me with a solid educational foundation while fostering my curiosity and encouraging me to explore topics beyond the standard curriculum. Their teaching has left a lasting impact, influencing my academic journey and my personal growth and approach to the world.

At the end of each school day, the teacher would select two students to assist with tidying up the classroom, and I always eagerly anticipated my turn. Armed with a broom, I meticulously swept the floor, raising clouds of dust that danced in the sunlight streaming through the windows. Our school, situated in a remote area, did not have the luxury of electricity or running water, and there were no restroom facilities. Instead, we made use of a portable toilet known as a latrine. This essentially comprised a hole in the ground, discreetly tucked away behind the building. Once the hole reached capacity, it was carefully covered with dirt, and the portable toilet was relocated to a fresh spot, a process that our small community cooperatively managed.

The fragile, almost transparent pages of the only book available in my grade were a gateway to a world of knowledge and wonder. Each page held the weight of the printing press ink, an imprint of the only source of information available to us. The book's delicate, white pages were adorned with captivating illustrations of exotic animals, taking me on an imaginary adventure to far-off lands. The portrayals of a bustling city, unfamiliar to me, ignited my curiosity and wonder.

The scarcity of books prompted me to become intimately familiar with my older sister Diolete's textbooks. I eagerly pored over her books, desiring to absorb the knowledge and insight they held. Over time, those cherished volumes became my own. Each year, I meticulously erased the penciled-in activities from her books, symbolizing the renewal of knowledge and the continuation of my education. Dressed in Diolete's worn and outgrown clothing, I pondered the inequities that marked my childhood.

Why me?
Why do I have to use her notebooks?
Why do I have to wear her worn clothes?

Those thoughts loomed large as I diligently erased each page, hoping for a future where I could access a wealth of educational resources of my own.

I used to eagerly anticipate lunchtime because it meant we would get to enjoy the most incredible soup made by our teacher's family. Each day, two lucky students, including myself on occasion, were chosen to embark on a short half-mile journey from the school to the teacher's home to retrieve a large pot filled with the most mouthwatering soup I had ever tasted. This simple yet flavorful dish comprising rice and an assortment of vegetables never failed to entice my taste buds. Even now, the memory of those delicious soups leaves me wishing for more.

For hours, the soup was meticulously prepared in a large, bubbling pot simmering on the wood stove. Transporting that boiling mixture back to the school presented a challenge. To prevent any spills, we ingeniously devised a method using a sturdy wooden plank to stabilize the pot. In the rare instance that we forgot the wooden support, we resorted to using the sides of our shirts as makeshift "kitchen gloves" to protect our hands from the searing heat.

The students brought chipped mugs, ready to savor every last drop of the delicious soup. Laughter filled the air as we enjoyed multiple helpings until the pot was empty. After our satisfying meal, we excitedly streamed out to the field, engaging in lively games of dodgeball, hide-and-seek, and soccer. As the ring of the bell echoed across the field, we reluctantly returned inside to continue with the activities in our books.

Without running water at the school, the teacher would bring in a substantial jug of water, which we all shared using a single glass. Surprisingly, the children seldom became sick. The well water from the farm probably contributed to strengthening our immune systems.

In the third and fourth grades, our curriculum included Portuguese, civics, geography, and math, with an additional focus on hygiene. A cartoon caught my attention during that time, reminding us to wash our hands after using the latrine, brush our teeth after meals, and shower daily. However, these instructions didn't align with my reality. The school lacked a proper plumbing system, making it impossible to follow the hand-washing guidance. At home, there was no bathroom; we relied on the forest behind our house; it was disgusting! I struggled to make sense of the cartoon's advice. I initially interpreted "showering every day" as a reference to rain, and I couldn't fathom how that was achievable since it didn't rain every day. The concept of brushing teeth was equally confusing; I was left pondering about the taste of toothpaste and its purpose. *Was it sweet? Was it sour? Could I eat it?* Those questions lingered until my teenage years when I finally experienced brushing my teeth with toothpaste for the first time.

Every morning and at the end of the lunch break, we would form a disciplined line, with each student placing their right hand on the right shoulder of the student in front of them. Then, in complete silence, we would proceed to our designated seats, which were double seats shared with another classmate. This practice instilled in us the value of cooperation and sharing.

The classroom protocol always demanded that we stand up in unison whenever a visitor walked in, regardless of who they were. Only after the guest requested us to resume our seats would we fall back into silence, diligently working on our assignments until the visitor's departure. Among the regular visitors were two distinctive ladies. One exuded youth and sophistication, always impeccably dressed with high heels, while the other, in contrast, was older, wore oversized eyeglasses and a wig, and had a liking for heavy makeup. Those ladies held the title of "city" supervisors, yet, their actual responsibilities remained a mystery to me, as they never seemed to address pressing issues such as getting new windows for the school or fixing any existing problems. I vividly recall longing for a pencil sharpener, a wish that was never fulfilled by those ladies. Instead, our teacher resorted to using a double-edged razor blade to sharpen our pencils, which occasionally resulting in minor finger cuts. At home, I salvaged my father's discarded razor blades from the trash, ensuring that I had a reliable tool to keep my pencils sharpened.

Almost every day during my first-grade year, the homework assignment was to cut out words with the specific letter we were learning that day from the packages of things we had at home, which, for me, were not much other than sugar, coffee, and flour. We also had to write an essay with the title given by the teacher, which was always something related to the farm, as we didn't know any aspect of life outside of the farm. I was passionate about learning. My father had one old book, and I was fascinated by it. It is the only book I remember having access to at home in my early years. When I learned to read, I memorized *Canção do Exílio* from that book, and I know it by heart to this day. *Canção do Exílio* is a poem written by the Brazilian Romantic author Gonçalves Dias in 1843 when he was in Portugal studying law at the University of Coimbra. The poem is a famous example of the first phase of Brazilian Romanticism, characterized by strong nationalism and patriotism.

On a beautiful day in second-grade, our teacher gave us an assignment to draw a house. I poured my heart into creating what I thought was the most beautiful house, only to have my teacher write a note that said, "Janete's barn." Although intended as a charming comment, it shattered me inside. To me, "barn" symbolized ugliness and desolation. It felt like confirmation that I was already living in a place resembling a barn. This experience left a lasting impact, as I still struggle to draw anything, including a simple barn. However, I deeply appreciate my siblings' diverse artistic talents and skills.

I always remember how my teacher regularly reminded my sister and me to ask our father for our birth certificates. Despite our efforts, when we inquired at home, we were dismayed to find out that there was a fee to be paid, and there was simply no money for it. This meant we were the only two children in our school without proof of our birthdays. This made me reflect on the absence of "happy birthday" songs in school, and it bothered me. It was later revealed that the lack of celebration wasn't due to the missing birth certificates but because my birthday fell in July when there were no classes. However, it took me a while to realize that my sister and I lacked this fundamental document proving our existence. I began worrying about the accuracy of my birthdate and name, as well as whether I could change them if I chose to. Those thoughts weighed heavily on my mind whenever the teacher brought up the issue. It wasn't until just before my sister completed the fourth grade that our father managed to obtain our birth certificates, which allowed her to enroll in fifth grade in the city. I was on the brink of turning eight when I was finally acknowledged as a member of society.

The Road

The rising dust clouds transformed my school uniform's once pristine white shirt into a worn brownish-yellow and settled on my perspiring face. The verdant, indigenous green trees lining the road took on a somber, dark yellow hue during the rainless days of summer. However, when the long-awaited rains finally arrived, the dust mixed with the water, forming a treacherous, slippery mud that made our school walks challenging. Despite our best efforts, the mud inevitably found its way onto our shoes and uniforms, yet we never used this as an excuse to miss class. My sister Diolete and I took great pride in our punctuality, and we rarely missed a school day.

The rural farm school provided education for students up to fourth grade, which prompted my parents to seek further schooling for my siblings and me. As a result, we were enrolled in a school in Mandirituba, a small town approximately forty-five kilometers from Curitiba, the capital of Paraná, my home state. It's about five kilometers from our farm. Mandirituba was created by State Law 4245 on July 25, 1960, which separated it from the city of Sao Jose do Pinhais, Paraná. In the seventies, the population of Mandirituba was about twelve thousand, and the economy was based on agriculture.

I vividly remember my time in fifth grade. Our school uniform was navy blue with two white stripes along the pants and sweater with a crisp white shirt underneath. It was a unifying factor for most students, except for the affluent kids who wore stylish shoes. My uniform, unfortunately, was made of poor-quality material, causing it to appear more purple than navy blue. To top it off, I wore a pair of sneakers known as congas, synonymous with poverty in our community. When other kids glanced at my feet, they instantly recognized my family's financial struggles. The shame was unbearable, so I distanced myself from the wealthy students and retreated to the back of the classroom.

I have so many cherished memories of my oldest sister, Diolete. Despite being shorter than me, she had a radiant beauty with her red hair and endearing freckles. She was a year ahead of me in school and had a tight-knit group of friends. During lunch breaks, I always sought her out and spent time with her and her friends.

During this time, a girl from my class named Angela noticed my routine and began sitting in front of me and spending time with me during breaks. Angela had a captivating smile that would light up the room every time she walked in. She always had a collection of colorful pens, pencils, and notebooks, which she generously shared with me to brighten up my own notebooks.

From fifth to eighth grade, I found myself frequently at Angela's house, especially when we were working on projects or preparing for exams. It's curious to note that I never had Angela over to my house, and I'm not even certain she knew where I lived. Despite this, I'm confident our friendship would have remained unchanged had she visited. Our bond extended past our school years, but as life often does, we eventually grew apart.

I hold Angela in high regard and dearly remember her last gesture of love when she lent me her stunning reddish-black dress for my high school graduation.

As a young child, I was often warned not to overhear adult conversations, but I couldn't help but overhear my grandma Bertula telling my mom how much she believed in my red-haired sister, Diolete. She expressed concern that I might get involved with boys and give up on my education. This confused me since our father prohibited my sister and me from interacting with boys. Despite this, I knew in my heart that I was attracted to boys, or at least one in particular. It was disheartening to hear my grandma's words, especially because I wasn't meant to hear them in the first place. However, I was determined to prove her wrong and demonstrate that I was just as intelligent as my sister.

One afternoon, a creative teenage notion sparked in my mind, and I decided to share it with my Grandma. Excitedly, I announced my plan to learn how to cut hair. To my surprise, Grandma enthusiastically volunteered to be my first customer. Overwhelmed with excitement and anxiety, I picked up a pair of silver scissors and carefully trimmed Grandma's delicate gray hair. My efforts deeply touched Grandma; from that moment on, she entrusted only me with her hair.

When it came to my Grandma, music, and dancing were more than just hobbies – they were sources of joy and freedom. She often shared that when she listened to music and danced, all her worries disappeared. When a melody started playing inside the house or out in the open, Grandma would gracefully start moving to the rhythm, a brilliant, heartfelt smile adorning her face. She used to express her wish to her children and grandchildren, saying, "When I pass away, I want a dance party around my casket." Reflecting on those cherished moments, I am convinced that music and dancing gave Grandma the comfort and strength to usher countless babies into the world.

My father always insisted that my sister Diolete and I never go out alone without Grandma as our chaperone. Grandma never failed to show up, donning a white bandanna around her head and keeping a straw cigarette tucked behind her ear. She would lovingly accompany us to church parties, walking for kilometers with us along the dirt road.

Grandma had been married three times and widowed three times, but she never shared the details of her married life with her grandchildren, perhaps thinking we were too young to understand. However, she often shared her hope that one of her grandchildren would choose a religious vocation, becoming a priest or nun. Almost every other day, she would ask my sister Diolete and me, "Are you planning to enter the convent? Grandma would be so pleased if you became a nun."

"We always answered, "No, Grandma."

The fulfillment of her dream came years after her death, when our cousin Claudemir became a priest, is truly remarkable and inspiring.

Grandma was an experienced midwife who had delivered numerous babies, including me and some of my siblings. Her deep understanding of natural remedies for various illnesses proved invaluable, especially concerning my well-being as a baby. According to my mom and my aunt Nucha, in my early days, I was merely skin and bones and cried incessantly. While my mother breastfed all her children, her milk did not suffice for me. I failed to grow or gain weight as expected for an infant. Grandma suggested that if my parents wished for me to thrive, they should switch to goat milk. Taking Grandma's advice, my dad acquired a goat to provide the nourishing milk I needed. I thrived on goat milk and continued drinking it until I was five. I still vividly recall the last time I sat beside my mom as she milked the goat, a routine that played a crucial role in my early years.

As I sat by Grandma's hospital bed just twenty-four hours before she passed away, she shared some invaluable advice with me. Knowing I had been in an unfulfilling relationship for years, she took my hand, gazed into my eyes, and said, "Remember, no one will prioritize your happiness but you. It's time to end this relationship, embrace your freedom, and savor life. What's meant for you will patiently be there waiting for you."

In her final wishes, Grandma asked her grandchildren to serve as pallbearers at her funeral. My siblings, cousins, and I gathered to fulfill this responsibility following Grandma's request. Together, we carefully carried her casket from her home to the church, a distance of about two hundred meters, along a dirt road. It was a somber yet meaningful journey as we honored and remembered our beloved grandmother.

The Farm

The daily routine began early in the morning. Without an alarm clock in the house, the incessant rooster crowing signaled that it was already five a.m. The rooster's crow pierced through the quiet morning air, signaling the dwindling minutes of precious sleep.

The soft, warm glow of the antique radio's dial caught my eye as I carefully adjusted the volume just below the level of the rooster's spirited morning call. I wanted to ensure that my younger siblings would continue to sleep peacefully. Something about the twang of country music seemed to light up those early mornings. It became the comforting soundtrack to my daily journey to school and the lively background music to my afternoons on the farm. There was a magic in those moments that I couldn't imagine ever replacing with anything else.

The morning routine was simple and comforting. I remember the feeling of splashing cold water on my face from the aluminum basin while my sister Diolete skillfully tended to the wood stove, filling the air with the aroma of brewing coffee. Our breakfast was modest, often just a cup of coffee and a slice of bread. Otherwise, we would wait for the school's meal during the 10 a.m. break.

The farmland was three kilometers from our house. The dirt road that led to the farm was lined with beautiful tall Pinheiros. The Pinheiros, also known as Brazilian pine or Paraná pine (Araucaria angustifolia), are native to South Brazil. The only sound was the rustle of their green leaves and the birds on their branches. My sister and I were always afraid of walking to the farmland after school. What would we do if a stranger emerged from the jungle in front of us? We often saw a jararaca snake, a highly venomous pit viper species, slithering across the street in front of us. We stood still and quiet, our hearts pounding like drums in our chests as we watched it continue on its way. The jararaca snake usually hunts at night and takes shelter in foliage during the day. My mom once told us that when a jararaca gets a headache, she hunts during the day, and it could kill if it bites. "If you see a jararaca, don't move. Just let it go, and you will be safe." Jararaca snakes are venomous, but the story about headaches was made up by my mom to prevent us from approaching the reptile. It was always frightening to encounter one crawling on the dirt road.

There was also the caninana snake; it can reach about 2.5 meters in length and is relatively fast. It is known for being agile and having a menu of animals much larger than its own body. The caninana snake is not poisonous; however, it is not peaceful and can be aggressive when feeling threatened, causing much damage. Potential prey can observe its visual signals when the snake is about to attack, as it will swell its neck and raise its front part in a sign of aggression. This behavior is considered threatening, causing other animals to run away in fear. If the caninana cannot avoid the fight, it will catch its prey by the neck for quick and efficient strangling. My siblings and I were told the true story of the caninana by Mom many times, and I was more afraid of being caught by it than being bitten by the jararaca. Whenever I saw a shining green caninana crawling on the road, I would think, *"Please don't jump on my neck. I don't want to die,"* holding my breath as my entire body sweated in fear, waiting for the reptile to disappear into the jungle.

As my sister Diolete and I made our way home from school, we were accompanied by other kids, and together, we walked for about forty-five minutes. Despite our shared journey, conversation among us was sparse, and for the most part, we walked in silence. On fair-weather days, the walk was a pleasant experience. However, when it rained, the five-kilometer path we took turned into a difficult, muddy road. As the rain continued to pour, it soaked our bodies, but rather than dampen our spirits, it led to lots of fun. We laughed at each other as we endeavored to protect our books and notebooks from getting wet. The rainy conditions stretched our journey, and what was typically a forty-five-minute walk transformed into over an hour as we navigated the downpour.

My sister and I had a close friend named Luis Henrique. He was the son of our first-grade teacher, and he and I were in the same grade. Our houses were on opposite sides of the farm, but not far away. We could see each other when walking down the hill each morning. The three of us would leave the house at 6:00 a.m. to arrive on time for the 7:10 a.m. class, which was the first one of the day. Our school allowed students ten minutes to get to class after the 7:10 a.m. bell. If someone was more than ten minutes late, they could still attend the first class, but they would already have received an absence note in the teacher's notebook.

Leaving home on time was essential for all of us, but sometimes we couldn't resist stealing a few extra minutes of sleep. Since we didn't have cell phones to stay in touch, we had to rely on our creativity. If we managed to leave on time, the sight of each other walking down the hill was always a reassuring sign. A few minutes later, we would meet at the street intersection and embark on our five-kilometer journey to school together. However, if we failed to spot each other, we had a clever solution. We would discreetly cut a tree branch and leave it at the corner of the intersection to signal to the others that we had already set off. This secret method of communication remained known only to the three of us.

Some of the kids from our school found the name Henrique to be quite funny and started teasing Luis Henrique by calling him just "Henrique." The name caught on, and soon, everyone started addressing him by this new nickname. Despite its origins, Henrique embraced it and became well-known by this name. Not only was Henrique a polite and composed individual, but he was also an exceptional student and a loyal companion to us all. He made sure that we always got home safely and looked out for us like a caring older brother would. My father held Henrique in high regard; despite being wary of boys spending time with his daughters, he trusted Henrique completely. Whenever we wanted to attend a school event, our first question was always directed at Henrique - if he was attending, it meant that we were likely to get permission from our dad. He made my father feel reassured, knowing that his daughters were safe in Henrique's company.

Because Henrique and I were always together, we often became victims of bullying from two of our classmates, Sandro and Pedro. Sandro and Pedro never acted alone; they always acted as a team. In class and inside the school building, they were respectful, and both were brilliant students. However, Pedro always scored an A+ while Sandro often cried when he didn't score an A+. As soon as we left the school gates and started walking home, Pedro and Sandro would quickly grab their bikes and ride past us, shouting, "Henrique is your husband! Henrique is your husband!" and "Janete is your wife! Janete is your wife!" Then they would bike away, and we would think they were gone. But no, they would come back and circle us, laughing and shouting, "Henrique is your husband! Henrique is your husband!" and "Janete is your wife! Janete is your wife!" We silently continued our journey, walking and hoping that they would bike away. Since they both lived in the city, they were in no rush to get home, so they biked back and forth, laughing and shouting at us until they couldn't follow us any longer.

We usually took a shortcut through the beautiful property of Mr. Afonso Lourenco, a land of beautiful pastures with a lovely pond in the middle, adorned with tall apple and pear trees. We were allowed to walk through his land as long as we kept the responsibility of closing the gates so his cattle wouldn't escape to the city. We were responsible kids and always followed the instructions and protocols.

We used to take the long route through the city on Fridays. There was always a chance of getting a ride home from someone. Farmers from the town would offer us a ride if they saw us walking from school, and we usually accepted. It was common and safe to get a ride from someone on the dirt road. They either knew our parents or were just doing a good deed. Sometimes, on our way, we would encounter those two bikers who would tease us by shouting, "Henrique is your husband! Janete is your wife!" They loved to follow us because it was their route home, so they didn't need to ride back and forth.

THE DIRT ROAD

I found the chanting in my ears unpleasant. Henrique always seemed uncomfortable with it too, but we never fought back. I wanted to yell at Sandro and tell him how terrible he looked when he cried because he didn't score enough to match Pedro's score, but I never did. I also wanted to yell at Pedro and tell him that I had a mother and he didn't. I knew that would deeply hurt him, and maybe make him stop bullying us, but I never did. If I had done that, I would be as repugnant as they were.

The same pattern continued throughout our entire eighth grade. Rainy days were a blessing for us because the bullies' relatives would pick them up from school. After all, they were rich kids. We preferred the rain to the taunting.

Whenever my sister and I would return home from school, we would quickly eat our lunch and then embark on a three-mile walk to our family's farmland, where we would work tirelessly until late afternoon. The work at the farm was always demanding, regardless of the season. I distinctly remember starting to help my parents on the farm when I was just five years old. As I grew older, I gradually took on more responsibilities, such as preparing the soil, meticulously planting the seeds, and diligently maintaining the farm. I wasn't alone in this, as I was fortunate to share these duties with my three siblings: Diolete, my oldest sister, and my younger brothers, Joao and Jair. This upbringing instilled within me a strong work ethic and a deep appreciation for the value of hard work.

My younger sister Arlete was one year younger than me. She often cared for our younger siblings, entertaining them under a tree and calling our mom when it was time for her to breastfeed.

When I was growing up, farming equipment such as tractors, harvesting machines, and soil irrigation machinery were considered extravagant luxuries reserved for the wealthiest farmers. My siblings and I would stand in awe as these powerful machines rumbled by our farm, their imposing presence leaving a lasting impression on us. Meanwhile, our farming methods relied on traditional tools—a simple wagon, two loyal horses, a sturdy plow, and a collection of hoes. With these basic implements, we painstakingly planted and tended various crops, including rows of golden corn, black beans, potatoes, and sweet potatoes.

During the boiling summer days on the farm, when the temperature soared above 30 degrees Celsius, time seemed to slow down to a crawl. Each second felt like an eternity as we worked tirelessly to cultivate the plants under the relentless heat. The sensation of joy was palpable as the wind provided a much-needed respite, refreshing our sweaty and fatigued bodies. The contrast in seasons was striking, as winter's biting cold brought a sharp sting to our cheeks, serving as a stark reminder of the harsh and unforgiving nature of the changing weather.

Before I was born, my father had a small brick-and-block business (Olaria de tijolo in Portuguese) with his brothers. Bricks and blocks were produced from clay and sold to construction companies, which used them to build walls, pavements, and other elements in masonry construction. This business was very common in my rural community at the time. Although I have only vague memories of this business, I recall mixing different clay types and making my own little bricks while he worked. I also recollect walking behind my mom as she carried a cart of bricks and put them on the shed shelves to dry.

After our family business fell, my father was burdened with debt, an aging car, and the motor that powered our brickmaking machine. It was a tough time for my parents as they were starting a family and living with my paternal grandmother. Several years later, my father decided to sell the old car and the motor. With the money he made from the sale, he was able to make a down payment on a striking 1962 white and sky-blue Chevrolet truck. This truck had a quirk - it would only run consistently if the tank was full, but most of the time, it wasn't. To meet the monthly installment for the truck, my father took on a job transporting wood logs from the forest to the sawmill in Mandirituba.

Without access to a machine, my dad relied on the help of two young workers to load the enormous logs onto the truck, which he then drove miles away to unload at the factory. Before unloading, he meticulously calculated the load size in cubic meters. As a child, my dad didn't have access to pens and would write with a red square pencil, a pencil he kept that produced large and distinctive handwriting. Watching him write down the numbers with that red square pencil after completing his mathematical calculations was always fascinating. Despite only having a third-grade education, my father was incredibly adept at math, a skill that has stayed with him throughout the years.

I recall rare occasions when I found myself running late for school. On such days, my father kindly offered to drive me in his truck. Strangely, rather than being grateful for the gesture, I silently prayed that none of my friends would spot me arriving in the old, worn-out truck. I would have preferred being late and walking to school than being seen in that unattractive vehicle. But my father always beamed with joy as he dropped me off at the school gates.

The small size of our farmland meant that the larger farms in our rural community always had work opportunities for us. Aware that my father owned a Chevrolet, farmers would enlist his help in transporting workers to their farms. He would go to our neighbors and ask who would be interested in picking potatoes the next day. In the early morning, ten to fifteen ready workers would assemble in front of our house, each carrying their lunch in plastic supermarket bags and wearing hats and long-sleeve shirts to shield themselves from the sun. As they piled into the back of the truck, a mix of young and old, there was lively chatter and laughter, setting the stage for a long and arduous day ahead at the farm.

Picking up the potatoes was physically demanding, but there was an element of enjoyment in it. It often turned into a friendly competition among us as we strived to pick more bags of potatoes than our neighbors. When noon approached, the tractor would stop, signaling a break for us. We would then gather on the dry ground, open our plastic lunch bags, and savor the cold black beans and rice that awaited us. Unfortunately, water was scarce, so I made it a point to fill a glass bottle with fresh, well water in the morning to bring with us. However, when I felt thirsty, the once-refreshing water had turned warm, similar to a cup of hot tea, but it was what had to quench my thirst and rehydrate my body. At the end of the exhausting day, the day's earnings from the number of bags of potatoes picked by my siblings, my mother, and myself went solely to my father. As a child, I couldn't comprehend why I never received any payment for my hard work. It frustrated me, and in those moments, I would silently affirm, "*One day, I will have my own money.*".

Because we had no electricity, at the end of a tiring day, we relied on the soft, warm glow of the kerosene lamp to illuminate our homework. Our mother watched over us, concerned about the potential fire hazard posed by the lamp. Exhausted from the day's activities, we often drifted off to sleep, our heads resting on our open books.

While laboring at the farm on a beautiful summer day, I made a life-changing decision. At around thirteen years old, a strong inner voice assured me I wouldn't remain in poverty. Walking alongside my sister to and from school and the farmland on that dirt road, I couldn't discern her thoughts, but my own were crystal clear. I envisioned a future where I wouldn't have to walk but would instead drive my car on that very road, free from the toils of farming.

I used to believe farming was a profession for individuals who did not pursue education. These thoughts were rooted in my teenage years when I would reluctantly complete my daily farm tasks. At that time, I longed to emulate Professor Antonio Lourenco, also known as Professor Toninho, in Mandirituba. He was not just a teacher to me but a mentor who taught me history and geography from the fifth grade to high school. His remarkable ability to teach these subjects without using a book set him apart. He became my hero, even though I didn't fully comprehend the meaning of heroism then. While I struggled to grasp the subject of geography, his history lessons left an indelible mark on me. Even today, I am swept back to Professor Toninho's classroom whenever I encounter historical facts in books or conversations. As I made the five-kilometer journey to school each day, I envisioned a future where I could pursue a profession and follow in the footsteps of my extraordinary teacher.

During the winter months in South America, the region experiences a chilly climate with frost, although snowfall is rare. The nighttime sky is a breathtaking sight adorned with a multitude of stars. I fondly recall peering through the cracks in the wall or opening the makeshift wooden window to behold the stars' splendor and the moon's serene presence. My siblings and I were fascinated by the idea that some stars resembled horoscope signs, and we often embarked on quests to locate them, although we never succeeded in our endeavors.

Our small house consisted of a kitchen, my parents' room, and another room for all of us. Instead of a door, there was only a curtain separating the rooms. We didn't have beds and slept on the floor alongside bed bugs. Our bed sheets were old clothes repurposed into pillows and comforters, and the mattress was made of dried husks and old clothing. My siblings and I shared our room with corn and black beans during the harvest season. Our beds were made on top of the corn that had been harvested. We often saw mice running, looking for food while we made our makeshift beds. In the middle of the night, we were awakened by my parents as they tried to contain a bedbug infestation on our "beds" with some spray. The spray caused itching in our throats, adding to the discomfort of the situation. The house kitchen had a wooden stove, a small table, a bench, and an old cabinet. We didn't have knives or forks, only spoons. Our water glasses were whatever containers came from the supermarket, and occasionally, my father would buy a can of tomato sauce for our Sunday lunch, which we then repurposed as a water glass. We didn't even have enough plates, so we took turns eating. The dishes were washed in a large dishpan, and the water was thrown out behind the house because we didn't have a plumbing system.

I recall our meals consisting of whatever we cultivated on the farm or what my mother grew in her vegetable garden. Consumption of red meat was considered a luxury and reserved for an occasional Sunday. Soda was a rare treat, only enjoyed on holidays if my mother and grandmother hadn't brewed their homemade beer. When we did have soda, it was a red beverage made of berries, and it tasted delicious.

For the holidays, we usually roasted pigs. That didn't happen often either because the pigs were usually raised to sell and make some money. It was so sad to prepare excellent meat for the neighbors and keep the organs for ourselves. Sometimes, the neighbors would slaughter a pig for themselves and send the intestines to our house. It felt like we were some garbage disposal every time my mom accepted those pig intestines. I felt disgusted helping my mom clean those large and small intestines. The pungent odor polluted the air as the waste was taken by squeezing the spiral-shaped intestines into the crystalline water stream.

I would throw lots of water into the pig intestines to ensure that all the filth was gone so that it would become a meal for us later. The last step was to place a stick inside the intestine to have it flipped inside out and then rewash it. Mom was always grateful for what she had, but she had a sad expression when she prepared those intestines.

The farm was the land of my paternal grandfather Leopoldino. He divided the property among his children before he died. I was a year old when he passed away. My mom often recalled the conversations she had with him days before he died. He predicted his grandchildren would live in a different world and that technology would soon arrive to change people's lives. Grandpa gave my dad the farmland, but the land does not produce money. It's necessary to plant and pray for the climate to be generous. Many times, it wasn't; either there was too much rain or no rain at all. Also, a supply and demand issue often affected the production at the farm.

During certain seasons, when the weather was less forgiving, we experienced considerable losses, especially with the beans, harvested in January, coinciding with the rainy season in South Brazil and making it particularly challenging. Lacking proper storage facilities, we suffered a complete loss of the harvest. When we experienced those losses, we counted on the help of a food program from the city. In Mandirituba, there was a food program that provided my mom with a monthly basket of essential items such as black beans, rice, powdered milk, and cornmeal. Every month, my mom would walk five kilometers on the dirt road with my siblings and me, carrying a big food bag. Upon arriving home, she would make polenta for us. At first, I didn't like polenta, but it was the only option to satisfy our hungry bodies, so I ate it without complaints, but for me, it was poor people's food. Corn was one of the products we always had. In fact, during rainy days, our jobs were to thresh corn all day or until our thumbs became blistered, and then we were rewarded with the corn cob to play with until it was used in the wooden stove to start a fire. After we threshed the corn, my mom would put it in a big bag, then put the bag on her back and walk five kilometers along the dirt road to exchange the corn for cornmeal and corn powder (which we call farinha). This way, we always had enough cornmeal to make polenta.

In the heart of the town center sat an old corn mill that ran on the power of water. Every time we visited, the kind owner would allow my siblings and me to observe the intricate process of the mill's water wheel powering two stones that processed the grains, turning them into flour, and cornmeal. We then enjoyed the corn powder with black beans, milk, and eggs. My mom always made sure that we were never hungry, sacrificing her own food to ensure her children were well-fed, sometimes with just a simple but comforting meal like polenta. Over time, I have cherished the taste of polenta, finding it satisfying and delicious. However, it wasn't until later in life, when I began attending formal dinners where polenta was served as a gourmet dish, that I was able to dissociate it from its initial association with poverty.

Christmas

I have few memories of playing with my siblings growing up, as we were all busy working on our family farm alongside our parents. Christmas was a special time for us, not because we received gifts, but because our parents taught us the true meaning of the holiday—that it commemorates the birth of Jesus, who came to save humanity. We didn't exchange Christmas gifts but took part in the tradition of novenas. In Roman Catholic tradition, novenas are a series of special prayers and worship services held nine days before Christmas. These observances helped us to reflect on the significance of Jesus' birth and to deepen our understanding of his role as our Redeemer, as described in the Bible and our Catholic beliefs.

During the enchanting nine nights leading up to Christmas, we would pray at our neighbor's house. There was something magical about walking in the moonlight or using a candle to navigate the darkness to reach our neighbors' homes. After our heartfelt prayers, the host graciously offered us delicious cakes, cookies, coffee, and sometimes even a small glass of liquor. When the gathering took place at our humble barn, we would offer a simple and warm welcome; that is what we had to offer. Despite this, our neighbors continued to grace us with their presence, gathering for prayers and fostering a sense of community and togetherness.

In early December, my siblings and I would excitedly venture into the forest, eagerly searching for a petite pinheiro tree to adorn. We would decorate it with great care and enthusiasm with whatever items we had on hand. During that time, the pinheiro trees were a common sight, their presence lending a touch of natural beauty to our surroundings. Among the diverse wildlife, the gralha-azul bird, a distinctive species native to the southern region of Brazil, particularly in my home state of Paraná, held a special significance. This remarkable bird was known for reintroducing the araucaria, the revered symbolic state tree of Paraná.

Legend has it that the bird has a sacred duty to help spread this tree. In the fall, groups of gralha-azul gather pine nuts (araucaria fruit) and bury them in the ground or in decaying tree stumps, which ultimately promotes the growth of new trees. Today, both the bird and the Pinheiro tree are at risk of extinction.

Christmas Eve held a special significance for us as it marked the anticipation of Jesus' arrival. Our tradition involved walking to the church, which stood just fifty meters from our house. The church, situated on land donated by my great-uncle Olimpio, held a deep personal connection to our family. My siblings and I eagerly participated in the Christmas play, followed by the magical experience of attending the midnight mass at Senhor Bom Jesus Church in Mandirituba, where we would happily walk five kilometers on the dirt road to attend the mass using lanterns made with wood sticks and candles covered with colorful film. It was marvelous to walk in the dark with those colorful homemade lanterns. The atmosphere was enchanting, with the melodic hymns, the twinkling lights of the Christmas tree, and the heartfelt performances in the Church. The joyous occasion continued as we savored a delightful meal together on Christmas Day.

Every year, my siblings and I anticipated the arrival of Santa Claus, the jolly old man who was said to bring gifts to children worldwide. However, despite our best efforts to behave well throughout the year, Santa never visited our house. On Christmas Day, we would excitedly check under the tree, hoping to find presents from him, but every time, our hopes were dashed. We started to question whether Santa even existed, especially since we knew he visited other children. Perhaps our humble house didn't meet his standards, or he overlooked us. Those feelings left us wondering why Santa didn't seem to care for us or understand our desires.

We started writing him letters to ask why he always skipped our house.

Was it because our house was ugly?

Was it because he didn't know what we wanted?

Was it because he didn't like us?

Was it because we didn't have nice clothes or beautiful shoes?

He always chose not to respond. We were not upset, maybe disappointed, as it was customary not to have much anyway.

Even though Santa forgot us, we knew Dona Alice wouldn't. Dona Alice was our neighbor, an elderly lovely woman that never forgot to bring candies for all the children in our community. The intricate map of wrinkles adorning Dona Alice's face bore witness to her extraordinary life's odyssey characterized by deep faith, incredible bravery, and boundless compassion. Framed by delicate lines, her eyes radiated warmth and affection as she bestowed candies upon the eager children on Christmas Day. After the reverent Christmas Day prayer, Dona Alice gathered the children around the church's altar, where we joined in prayer, lifted our voices in joyful Christmas songs, and engaged in heartfelt discussions about the profound significance of the birth of Jesus. The sensation of receiving those delightful candies from Dona Alice remains imprinted in my memory as a marvelous and unforgettable experience.

Apart from my family, I miss so many things about Brazil. One surprising thing is how much I miss the community and spirituality I experienced at the small church just in front of my house. I miss the warmth of the Sunday prayers, the sense of belonging, and the spiritual growth from attending religious retreats.

Dona Alice made it a regular practice to take my sister Diolete and me to various spiritual weekend retreats, providing us with invaluable opportunities to disconnect from the world's chaos and immerse ourselves in prayerful contemplation. Her constant presence in the church, where she fervently conveyed the teachings of the Word of God to all, was truly inspiring. When she graced the church altar with her uplifting words, it was as if she composed a beautiful symphony that resonated with everyone in attendance. Dona Alice's extraordinary gifts left an indelible mark on our hearts. I will always cherish her for the Christmas candies she shared and for being a shining example of faith, incredible commitment, and a fervent desire to foster growth within our community.

In our family, Christmas remains a meaningful celebration of the birth of Jesus. We've upheld the tradition of forgoing gift exchanges in favor of a beautiful meal, shared laughter, and heartfelt appreciation for one another's presence.

My Father

Dad was distant from his children, rarely showing warmth and affection. I often saw other fathers hugging their kids when they dropped them off at school, displaying a beautiful scenario of love, affection, and pride. However, I never experienced this with my father. I grew up not knowing how it felt to be embraced by him. I longed to lean my ears on Dad's chest and hear the beating of his heart, but I never did.

I remember seeing Dad holding my younger siblings as babies in his arms and dancing with them on the kitchen floor. I wondered if he did that with me, too. Mom said he did, but as we grew up, there was this barrier between us. I could not comprehend it until I understood that one cannot give what one never had.

Dad set a great example for us by emphasizing the importance of hard work, attending church, and being a good person. He showed us the difference between someone who helps those in need and someone who does nothing.

Dad was incredibly empathetic and always willing to help others. He often brought homeless people to our little house and provided them with food. One night, we were awakened by the screams of someone lost around the farm.

My dad grabbed the flashlight and yelled at the stranger, "Who are you?" The stranger did not answer, so Dad inquired, "Are you armed?"

"I am not," said the stranger.

Still talking from a distance and with the flashlight, my father asked, "Where are you coming from, and where are you going?"

The stranger said, "I am lost and hungry."

If one thing melted my father's heart, it was to hear that someone was hungry. Dad invited the stranger in. We gathered in the kitchen while my father warmed up some beans and rice in the wood stove to feed the stranger. The stranger proceeded to ask my father if he would have a place for him to sleep that night. Without hesitation, my father made a bed with some old clothes on the kitchen floor and let the stranger sleep there for the night. Dad told the stranger not to scare his children and leave early in the morning. The stranger was gone when we woke that morning, and we never knew who he was.

Dad believed in the Bible, especially Mathew 25:35–36 (NIV): "For I was hungry and you gave me something to eat, I was thirsty and you gave me something to drink, I was a stranger and you invited me in, I needed clothes and you clothed me, I was sick and you looked after me, I was in prison and you came to visit me."

Dad always emphasized the importance of helping those in need, no matter how little we have to offer. The memory of the 1984 season is etched in my mind. Our small town was inundated with rain, leading to the loss of all our planted crops. Dad caught wind on the radio about the community's urgent need for food and clothing. Without a moment's hesitation, he enlisted the help of our neighbor, Mr. Chico Moura, and together, they traversed the neighborhood, diligently gathering an abundance of food. I vividly recall seeing Dad returning home, triumphantly carrying a large, white sack overflowing with essentials. Later that day, he selflessly drove to the donation center and delivered all the collected items, providing much-needed relief to those in distress.

My dad was a hardworking man who wore many hats - farmer, mechanic, and driver, to name a few. He was determined to put food on the table for our family, often sacrificing his comfort. As a child, I remember that Dad never indulged in buying new clothes or shoes for himself. Instead, he walked around in well-worn flip-flops and relied on hand-me-downs from family members. He prioritized providing for his children over spending on himself.

He married my mother, Filomena, and they were blessed with eleven children. Their first child was born, but unfortunately, he passed away just one month later. This heartbreaking event deeply affected the young couple as they started their family journey.

My father had an extraordinary talent for mathematics. He could solve complex equations without a calculator, even though he had only completed the third grade. He used to playfully tease us for using calculators for even the most straightforward math problems. Although I loved mathematics in school, I could never quite match my father's skills. I often relied on a calculator, which disappointed him. He aspired to become a mechanic and pursued this passion by reading books given to him by a friend. I vividly remember watching him studying those books when I was younger, igniting a profound appreciation for exploring new fields of knowledge.

He eventually became a mechanic, not as a profession, but to work on his truck or help other people. Our home was often a refuge for distressed people, as they would come at all hours seeking his expertise when their cars broke down. Despite the late hours, he never hesitated to lend a hand. One day, my mom asked why he was not charging those people. He answered, "One day, it could be one of my kids in need, and I would like someone to help." I never forgot those words, which would later prove true in my life.

We are a devout Catholic family, and one day, my dad decided to embark on the ambitious journey of reading the entire Bible within a month. The Bible he chose was a cherished heirloom, possibly dating back to the 1800s, and it was believed to belong to our great-great-grandfather. Despite its yellowed pages, he devoted hours daily to the ancient text, absorbing its wisdom and beauty. He made notes in the margins, underlining passages that spoke to his soul. Upon completing this monumental task, he felt a deep sense of accomplishment and often engaged in heartfelt discussions about the Biblical passages that had profoundly impacted him.

His fascination with the Book of Revelations and its prophetic verses became the focus of many of these discussions. When Pope John Paul II made his inaugural visit to Brazil in 1980, Dad was inspired to undertake a 1,222-kilometer pilgrimage to the City of Aparecida in the State of São Paulo, where he sought the Pope's words of wisdom and faith. The journey was arduous but filled with spiritual significance, and it left an indelible mark on him. Since that transformative pilgrimage, it has become a cherished tradition for my family to make an annual pilgrimage to the Sanctuary of Aparecida, honoring Our Lady Aparecida, the revered patroness of Brazil. The journey holds deep spiritual significance for each family member, nurturing a strong bond of faith among us.

After a long day's work, my father would partake in alcohol, which would transform him into a horrifyingly aggressive version of himself. It didn't take much; a mere sip would make him inebriated. When sober, he was the embodiment of serenity, never once raising his voice, even in the face of disagreement. However, under the influence, he would make threats and become belligerent. His drunken ramblings were more potent than the alcohol itself. It was a stark contrast to witness the man of faith succumb to a seemingly demoniac influence as the alcohol poured through his veins. His encounters with the devil on his way home were frequently described in disturbing terms, leaving me petrified. I found myself desperately praying for the sinister entity that was tormenting him to loosen its grip and set him free.

My father had never been aggressive towards my mother, but unfortunately, his behavior towards us, his children, was a different story. We could sense whether he was sober or drunk whenever his footsteps approached. We huddled together, pretending to sleep, hoping to avoid confrontation. My mother always displayed resilient strength, bearing the weight of the nonsensical and hurtful words that poured out of his mouth, words that would have never surfaced if it weren't for his alcohol consumption.

My mom dealt with him patiently and courageously to protect us. Sometimes, we were caught off guard and had to do things out of the ordinary, like washing his feet while he mumbled incoherently. One night, he came home while we were praying the Rosary, a practice our family still does at home. The Rosary consists of a chain with five sets of beads, with one large bead and ten small beads between each set. The large bead is separated from the smaller beads, signifying the different prayers recited while holding the bead. One bead followed by a group of ten is called a decade. When we gathered to pray the Rosary, we would pass the Rosary around, and one person would pray the first half of the ten beads to the Holy Mary, and then everyone else would pray the other half. Then, the Rosary would go to the next person, and so on, until the Rosary prayer was completed.

One disgraceful night, my father arrived home intoxicated while we were praying. He sat down quietly, just observing us. As we passed the rosary to one of my brothers, who was a little boy, he refused to pray the decade of the rosary. My father became very aggressive, grabbed the whip, and started beating up my brother while we continued praying in fear that one of us would be the next prey of the demon that attacked my father. The fury was so intense that no matter how much my mom implored him to stop hitting my brother, he wouldn't. We finished praying the Rosary amid his shouting. It was as though an evil spirit possessed him. The next day, he didn't remember anything.

Years earlier, I was a victim of my father's alcoholism. I was six years old. It was a Sunday afternoon, and my sister Diolete and I had fought. I threw a peach pit at my sister's forehead and made her cry, but five minutes later, we were playing again as if nothing had happened; in fact, that afternoon was one of the few memories I have of playing with my siblings when we were little. My father heard the story from Grandma, and since my sister Diolete was Grandma's favorite, Dad arrived home drunk that afternoon and started beating me. I remember watching my father removing his belt as he neared our house while I sat on the grass with my sister in front of the house. He whipped my entire body. He hit me with so much anger that if it weren't for my mother intervening, he would probably have broken my bones that afternoon.

I did not go to school the next day as my body was bruised and sore. I hated my father for the longest time. I could not look at him. I wanted him out of my life, but Mom explained that Dad wouldn't hurt me if it weren't for his disease. I never understood when my father said he did not remember anything. How was that possible? I honestly had an abominable feeling toward alcohol. It was the cause of emotional pain in my family. But in my mind, I wanted to try it just once and prove my father wrong. At the same time, the fear of becoming an alcoholic like my father has prevented me from trying it, and through the years, I have understood that alcohol had impaired my father's reasoning and memory.

I was in my late teenage years when he stopped drinking. I don't know if it was for medical reasons or because he felt it would be a disgrace for his children, now in their teenage years, to witness their father imbibe around the small rural community where everyone knew everyone. I will never know the answer.

During his alcoholism (alcoholic) years, he had never suffered any injury, but during his sober years, he would be a victim of several accidents. He had an injury in his eyes twice while cutting firewood—first the left, then the right eye, almost losing his vision for good—but God gave him back the blessing of seeing the world again and living and experiencing the good and the bad that was reserved for him in the years to come.

He was blessed with his first grandchild in October of 1998, a baby boy who was named Emerson.

In January of 2005 was the first wedding of one of his children, and in May of the same year was the tragic loss of one of his sons at the age of twenty-seven to a horrific truck accident while working cross-country in Brazil. This was the second time he would experience the terrible feelings of losing a child. This event left him with severe depression and with a broken heart.

In 2006, another child got married. But in the same year, My Father got into a car accident that left him in the ICU for thirty days, but his strong will to live made him survive. After months of intense physical therapy, he started walking again, but the accident triggered his depression again.

In 2009, walking with difficulty and being very emotional, he walked me down the aisle in Brazil, and that was the last time he walked. After my wedding, he was back to bed, and in 2012, he was diagnosed with thrombosis in his right leg. Due to the severity of the diagnosis, his leg had to be amputated.

He was now in between the bed and the wheelchair. He became a child for my mom, but he was still conscious and recognized all his children and grandchildren, even though he couldn't discuss any subject. He even recognized my husband, who was a stranger in the family. When he first met my husband, Nick, in 2009, he was so happy to hear that Nick likes cars and enjoys fixing them like he did. He could not communicate with Nick due to the language barrier, but his expression of love and admiration was undeniable. I do not doubt that he had accepted Nick as part of our family and would love him like one of his children. Every time we spoke on the phone, he asked how Nick was doing.

I wish I had understood what was happening in my father's mind. I often did not understand him, thought he was too severe to us, and didn't let us do what we wanted. Today, I understand how much love and care a humble man gave his children—teaching respect, honesty, loyalty, compassion, and hard work. He worked to make sure that we had food at the table. Sometimes, he didn't have enough money to buy a kilo of something and would buy a quart of it until he could make more money to go to the grocery store. We had very little, just what was necessary to survive.

My father truly believed you can succeed through education and hard work. Nobody can diminish you when you are educated, no matter how simple you are. I am living proof of that.

Teenage Years

During my teenage years, "angry" didn't begin to describe how I felt. I experienced misery as a young woman growing up in a house without a bathroom, electricity, TV, or even a bed. Needless to say, I didn't have a bedroom of my own, and most importantly, we had no money. In a moment of defiance, I rebelliously convinced myself that I must have been adopted. Despite being raised in the same household, I couldn't help but feel like I didn't truly belong as my parents' biological child. This feeling of alienation led me to believe that I was fundamentally different and somehow didn't fit into the family or the particular circumstances of our lives, marked by poverty. The lack of physical resemblance to my siblings or parents only deepened my sense of being out of place.

The farm where I lived was a challenging place to be, especially during the summer months. The scorching heat, with temperatures often reaching 30 degrees Celsius, made it incredibly tough to work outside. On one particular afternoon, my mom, my siblings, and I were coming home from the farm when the sky suddenly turned an ominous, dark gray. The air grew heavy and tense, and the strong thunder shook the very ground beneath our feet. As we began our journey home, the rain poured down relentlessly, enveloping us in its cold embrace. The darkness made it difficult to navigate, but sudden bursts of lightning illuminated the path before us, revealing the shattered outlines of tree limbs strewn about. Our clothes clung to our bodies, soaked from the unrelenting downpour, and each step forward felt like a battle against the elements. As we neared our house, the rain came to a stop, and we were able to discern the extent of the damage caused by the strong wind to our modest home. I vividly remember that terrifying day when we rushed back home with a sinking feeling in my stomach. The sight of our house's roof completely destroyed was both terrifying and confusing. All that mattered at that moment was the safety of my sister, Diolete, and my baby brother, Jose Luis, who had been home that day. As we frantically searched, we found my sister sheltering the baby in a fragile corner of the house that miraculously remained intact amidst the chaos. Witnessing my sister in tears while holding on to my brother was a heart-wrenching moment. It felt as if the hand of God had shielded us from the worst on that fateful day.

In the aftermath of this disturbing incident, I embraced the hard task of helping my parents cultivate corn, black beans, and sweet potatoes. Despite the physical exhaustion, my mind often drifted to distant aspirations. I envisioned myself in a sophisticated office, seated behind an exquisite mahogany desk, occupied in important conversations over the telephone, wearing a pair of glasses, and smoking a cigarette. The stark contrast between this daydream and the reality of our rural life only fueled my determination to strive for a different path.

When I was thirteen years old, I vividly remember the day when I was sifting through old family photographs. It was at that moment that I noticed the striking resemblance between myself, my father, and my siblings. It was a profound realization, and it made me see the beauty of our family despite our difficult circumstances. Even though we were living in poverty, I made a personal commitment that I would no longer lament our situation.

But the intense feelings of anger and frustration persisted within me. When these emotions overwhelmed me, I sought solace in finding a large stone and breaking objects to release my frustration. The source of my frustration stemmed from the difficult financial circumstances my family faced, as well as the strain caused by my mother's frequent pregnancies. Furthermore, I was deeply troubled by the fact that I did not have access to menstrual pads when I experienced my menstrual period. This lack of access to proper menstrual hygiene products was a source of great distress for me. My older sister and I only had a small piece of fabric to manage our menstrual cycles, and we had to wash and reuse it each month. Also working on the farm, the lack of a bathroom or shower meant I could never properly clean myself after a long day's work.

It was a bright day on the farm when I heard a mysterious voice that seemed to spark a determination within me. At that moment, I made a solemn vow to myself that I would not accept a life of poverty. I remembered my father's words about the value of education, and from that day on, I knew that pursuing an education would be my ticket to a better future, no matter the obstacles I might face.

I looked up to my father as my source of inspiration. I remember observing him diligently reading the Bible and immersing himself in books to master the skills of a mechanic. Witnessing his ability to become a proficient mechanic without any formal schooling made me question why I couldn't achieve success when I had the opportunity to pursue education.?

Leaving the Farm

I was fourteen years old. I had finished eighth grade a year before. High school classes were offered in the evening only, and walking five kilometers on foot on a dirt road late at night to go home after classes would be challenging as no public street lights existed. The dream of continuing my education was on hold. My family's economic conditions were getting complicated, as the farm was not generating sufficient income to lift my family out of poverty.

My godmother Marta was a pure soul who would come to rescue someone in need and bring out the best in them. Her kindness, love, compassion, and beautiful smile illuminated people's lives. She knew my family's situation and started looking for a job for me. She introduced me to the Gelenski family, one of the richest in Mandirituba. Mr. and Mrs. Gelenski were of Polish descent. In their early life, they had been poor like me. Mr. Gelenski once told me his fascinating life story: he started working at fifteen at the only local bakery in Mandirituba called Panificadora do Jose Schueda. At eighteen, he served in the Brazilian Army as a sergeant, saved all the money he made in the military, and started his own business fixing wagons. Fast-forward to today, the Gelenski family owns a company that has been operating in the manufacturing machines market since 1966 for the most diverse industrial sectors, specializing in the production of machines for several sectors, including ceramics, grains, and laboratories in Brazil, Peru, and Angola.

I got a job as a live-in housekeeper and babysitter for Nene. Nene was two years older than me, with the appearance of a young child. Nene was born mute. Even though I had several siblings, I had never babysat them. I lacked the skills to care for my young siblings. I loved them, but honestly, I had no patience with their crying and whining. And there I was, babysitting a child with special needs. Although I was a child myself, I took the responsibility very seriously. I understood how important it was to care for Nene and help my family financially.

The house was a mansion for a small city like Mandirituba, with a large and gorgeous garden of wild pink, ivory, red, and yellow roses that made everyone turn their heads to admire as they passed. The fragrance from that magnificent garden gently drifted through the open windows and created a floral scent in the house. While cleaning the patio, I watched the birds and butterflies attracted to the roses, which stood out as the sunlight played off their petals.

Nene always understood my words in his own way. Sometimes, he would eat alone, and other times, I had to feed him. He couldn't eat anything unless it was blended because he was unable to chew. With patience, he was able to learn things. I taught him to clasp his shirt sleeves with his hand so that the sleeves would not ride up his arms when he wore his sweater. It sounds simple, but it was hard for him to comprehend, but he learned it. And he still does it to this day. We couldn't communicate verbally, but we still had fun together.

We were both deeply irritated by the relentless squawking of the parrot Loro, who resided outside our window. Loro seemed to be privy to every bit of information and familiar with everyone in the house. It was astonishing how annoying that bird could be, yet we found ourselves missing its presence on the rare quiet days. There were moments when Nene would gaze at the ceiling and burst into laughter, and I would laugh with him. While I couldn't discern any cause for amusement, it seemed like Nene had quite a few imaginary friends, who would often congregate and entertain him with tales. We were great pals, and I felt like I understood him perfectly.

The Gelenski's house was built years before with large bedrooms and a beautiful kitchen with an exotic round wooden table with a rotating disc in the middle that one activated by pressing an electric button, and the food would be brought where you were at the table. It was all created by Mr. Gelenski.

The kitchen had a hammock where Nene and I used to relax after meals. In the family room, there was a color TV, a luxury that only rich people could afford at the time. It was April 15th, 1986, and I had the TV on while I cleaned the room. The headline on the news read, "Reagan attacks Libya." The news of war terrified me. I had read about the horrific stories of the Pearl Harbor attack by the Japanese and the United States atomic bomb in Nagasaki and Hiroshima during the Second World War. I had seen a picture of a little Japanese girl after the bomb attack, and that image kept replaying in my mind as the discussion about Libya's attack went on. Over the years, I have heard many stories about wars, and each time I read a headline about war, my memory goes back to that particular day at Gelenski's house.

The bathrooms and shower at Gelenski's house were something I had never experienced before, and I enjoyed those comforts five days a week. In the shower, the water flowed down my body, providing a soothing sensation that I was only used to feeling from the rain. I felt joyful for a moment, but then a cloud of sadness invaded my soul as I remembered that my family was at home, heating water on the woodstove and using the aluminum water basin to wash their tired bodies. I wished I could have brought them all to Gelenski's house so they could experience the luxury of a hot shower.

The Gelenskis had five children, two of whom were already married. Over time, I developed a strong bond with all of the Gelenski children; in fact, some of them are still my closest friends.

During the weekdays, I was at the Gelenski's, on weekends, I went back to my parents' house and shared a bed with my sisters and a room with my brothers. It felt like living two different lives. During the week, I lived in a mansion, enjoying the comfort of a shower, my own bedroom, good food, color TV, meeting new people, and experiencing an affluent lifestyle. On weekends, I lived poorly, sharing a bed with my sister and a bedroom with all my siblings. It was a mix of emotions, but I knew that I was working off the farm to earn money and help my parents build a house.

After meticulously cleaning up after our dinner, I assisted Mrs. Gelenski in putting Nene to bed, ensuring he was comfortable and ready for a peaceful night's sleep. Meanwhile, Mr. Gelenski picked up his beloved accordion and filled the air with vibrant, traditional tunes. Despite his skillful performance, Mrs. Gelenski would affectionately tease him, playfully claiming that he was clueless about his musical skills. As the music filled the room, Mrs. Gelenski invited me to join her at the table where she unveiled a collection of vibrant art supplies. We spent hours joyfully doodling houses and flowers. Amidst laughter and shared creativity, we endearingly christened ourselves the "Picassos" of Mandirituba.

It's been several decades, and I've never felt the need to inquire about Nene's real name. To me, he will always be Nene. What strikes me is how, even to this day, he can identify me solely by the scent of my wrist. Whenever I make my way to Brazil, visiting the Gelenski family is a must. Upon my arrival at their home, Nene greets me by taking hold of my wrist, breathing in its scent, lightly tapping my wrist beneath his chin three times, and then breaking into a warm, knowing smile. At that moment, it's as though he has no doubt that it's me.

It's heartbreaking to know that he won't be able to read these words, but I find comfort in the fact that he has taught me the true essence of unconditional love and patience. I've grown to be patient with myself, my family, and the unpredictable nature of life. Through the days I spent with Nene, caring for him and understanding his needs, I left behind my anger and discovered a calm and patient side of myself that still resides within me. My journey into adulthood began at the age of fourteen, thanks to a mute child who taught me invaluable lessons that no perfect person ever could.

High School

I had been working at the Gelenski house for about a year when a high school class opened in the morning in Mandirituba. A three-year program called Magisterio trained students to become teachers from first to fourth grade. I did not think twice and enrolled in the class. I returned to my parents' house, and that year, I started working in the afternoons at a local store. Then, I would walk my five kilometers on the dirt road late in the afternoon to return home.

The classes were intense and required lots of studying. My classmates were all women, some my age, some older than me. My best friend Cida was my neighbor and was in my class. Cida and I were in the same class from first to fourth grade, and we met again in the Magisterio class. We spent lots of time studying for exams and preparing projects together. She was brilliant and always helped me with subjects I didn't understand, and I would help her with my math skills when she encountered difficulties. We were a good team.

The classes were taught at the exact location where I had finished eighth grade two years before, and the school administration had added brand-new rooms to the building to accommodate this new class. There was excitement in the air, as at the end of three years, we would be the first class of teachers to graduate in Mandirituba.

The program covered physics, Portuguese, math, psychology, and other subjects. We learned everything from Maria Montessori to Sigmund Freud.

Since the first year, we were required to observe other teachers in different schools and learn their methodology. The schools were all far away from my home. I was once assigned to observe a teacher

THE DIRT ROAD

in a rural community called Colonia Matos. I took the school bus to get to the school, but there was no bus or any other type of transportation to come back late in the afternoon, so I walked about twelve kilometers to return home late in the afternoon.

I enjoyed walking back and forth everywhere. I was a fast walker. My colleagues didn't enjoy walking along with me that much. Since I was fast, I decided to use that skill in sports. I started participating in track and field during my school years. I was always involved in competitions; I won several first-place medals in running, high jump, and distance jump. Only one time, I got second place in the high jump, which I still resent to this day—that silver medal between the gold ones.

I was unaware of my ability to play sports until I started participating in the Sports Week events at my school. The event was held in September of every year, and I always looked forward to it and participated in those events from fifth grade to high school. My physical and mental training was done through walking back and forth to school and the farm. Sometimes, I had to go to the farm by myself, and as much as I wanted to be courageous, I was terrified of walking alone, but I wouldn't let anyone know. Instead of being the victim of my fear, I started running so I wouldn't think about encountering a stranger along the road or a snake. In my mind, those encounters could happen, but there was no way anyone or any reptile could catch me if I were running, and that's how I became fearless. I don't fear the unknown. I love challenges, and I am a risk-taker. I was pretty surprised each time I secured first place. There were always many competitors; they all looked good in their sports uniforms, T-shirts with numbers on the back, matching shorts, and athletic shoes while I had my navy-blue school uniform and a pair of congas to compete, but I enjoyed the excitement.

In 1992, two years after I had graduated from high school, I decided to run the Saint Silvester Marathon in São Paulo, Brazil. Its course is fifteen kilometers long. It's less than half of the length of a marathon, but the race is intense due to the summer heat and the geographic obstacles. The event occurs on December 31 each year. That year, I took the bus from Curitiba, and five hours later, I arrived in São Paulo, ready for the run. I finished the race, got the bus back to Curitiba around 11:00 p.m. that night, and celebrated New Year's Eve with other athletes like me on the bus. I had just checked off one of the items on my bucket list.

During my second year of high school, there was a shortage of first-grade teachers in Fazenda Rio Grande. Mandirituba's secretary of education, Angela N., was my teacher and asked me if I would take the challenge and start teaching. I said yes and was given a class with thirty-eight first graders. I was seventeen in a classroom with the poorest children in town.

Poverty was not strange for me, but my students belonged to a level of poverty much more severe than my own. They would come to class with all kinds of problems, from alcoholic parents to physical and mental abuse. After being worn for weeks, the odor of their clothes was strong, making it impossible to close the classroom door. Their heads were full of lice, which infested my hair many times, but that was not strange to me either.

My head had been infested with lice several times. Whenever my siblings and I got lice, my father would spray a pesticide named BHC (hexachlorobenzene) on our heads and wrap it up with a piece of fabric before we went to bed. There was a race of lice running on my head as they took their last breath before dying on my scalp. As I washed my hair with hot water and soap in the morning, I couldn't believe how rapidly they had multiplied. The smell was awful, and I don't know how no one died from the use of this chemical. Sometimes, my father cut my and my sister's hair short and shaved my brother's head to contain the spread. The use of this pesticide is now banned in Brazil.

Many kids needed attention due to their environment. I was always conscious of the lack of affection and love in their household, so I did my best to teach them to read and write and, above all, make them feel loved and appreciated for every bit of progress they made in class. I adored teaching. It was my best reward when most of them could advance to second grade at the end of the year.

Paulinho was my favorite student. He was short and skinny. He parted his blond hair to his right, looking like a little man in his orange sweater and black boots. Paulinho had difficulty learning, but I could tell he desired to learn. All he needed was extra love to improve. I spent time with him and appreciated every little improvement he made. Years earlier, I had learned with Nene to be patient and kind, and there it was, in front of me, the opportunity to make a difference. As time went by during the year, Paulinho started writing the words perfectly and developed the most beautiful handwriting skills. His notebook symbolized perfection for a first grader, and soon after, Paulinho surprised me when he looked at my desk and started reading a page I hadn't even started teaching yet. I was elated when Paulinho took the final test and scored high enough to move on to second grade.

Fazenda Rio Grande was thirty minutes by bus from Mandirituba. At the time, the City of Mandirituba offered a free bus ride to the population to travel from Mandirituba to Curitiba. Since Fazenda Rio Grande was between the two cities, I could take the free transportation to work when I could fit in the overcrowded bus with people taking advantage of the free ride and sometimes fighting over a seat. The bus carried twice the permitted capacity—a mix of women, men, and children, tightly packed like sardines. When a passenger in the middle of the crowded bus needed to disembark, it would require several people to exit, allowing the passenger to step out, and then everyone would board the bus again. Occasionally, that person in the middle happened to be me.

My classes ended at noon, and I ran to take the bus and arrive on time to teach my class at 1:00 p.m. at Escola Progresso. Not knowing anyone at the school was a challenge for me. I was a teenager, and obviously, I did not have enough experience in the classroom. As I started working, I presented myself with all kinds of questions.

Can I teach?

Would I encounter anyone willing to help me should I ever need it?

How about if the kids don't learn anything due to my lack of experience?

Would I make a difference?

All those questions haunted me, but I wanted to prove I could do it. Danuzia D. was the director of Escola Progresso. She was known as a rugged individual. I was concerned about my interaction with her due to my lack of experience. Still, contrary to what I had heard, I only experienced kindness from Danuzia. She was always available to help me with my classroom needs and discuss issues regarding my students, and she cared about my well-being.

Great friendships were born at Escola Progresso. All the teachers were great people, but Sandra and Adriane were exceptional and they were teenagers like me. We started getting to know each other and discovered much in common. Adriane lived three blocks from school and often would bring me to her house for coffee while I waited for my overloaded bus to return to Mandirituba. While we had coffee, we shared teenage stories and more mature conversations about work, our students, and life. Dona Landa, Adriane's mom, a tall, classy, and sophisticated woman with a joyous personality, always surprised us each time with a new joke, making us crack up at the table.

On weekends, I would spend time at Sandra's house. Sandra and I had a lot to talk about. Our teen stories were so important to discuss that we couldn't fall asleep and often found ourselves back in the kitchen at 3:00 a.m., eating again.

Our enduring friendship serves as a powerful testimony to the unbreakable nature of true friendship. We have had numerous challenging experiences, confronting emotional pain, frustration, and sadness, and yet our bond has only strengthened, keeping us even closer together. Furthermore, we have also created countless precious memories filled with laughter and shared unique experiences over the years.

On the journey back to Mandirituba, the situation was even more challenging as everyone was sweating profusely after a long day. Teachers in Brazil were and still are not adequately compensated, so I had to take the overcrowded bus because I couldn't afford the fare. I don't recall the exact amount I earned, but I know that if I had to pay for the bus, I wouldn't have much left to support my parents.

I would arrive in Mandirituba around 6:30 p.m. Walking the five kilometers alone in the evening could be risky since the dirt road didn't have any public lighting. I would need my father or one of my siblings to come to the bus station and accompany me back home.

I decided to enroll in a second high school class in the evening: accounting. I was in my second year of teaching school in the morning and my first year of accounting in the evening. As the city offered free rides to people to ride back and forth to do nothing, they also offered a free bus ride to take the kids back to the farm in the evening after classes. In doing that, I left home at 6:30 a.m. and came back home at midnight. After arriving home, I had to prepare my teaching lessons for the next day, study for my morning class, and do my homework for both.

In my third year of high school, the bank Bamerindus or HSBC Bank, opened a branch in a building owned by the Gelenski family. When the manager asked for a referral from Mr. Gelenski, I was the first one he recommended for a position. I also had to take a written test, which I did well on.

The grand opening of a new bank caused quite a stir in Mandirituba. The small city was buzzing with excitement as new businesses arrived in the area. I made sure to dress the part for my job—I wore a pair of tailored navy trousers, a crisp white shirt, and a navy blue jacket. I felt confident in my attire, but little did I know that an embarrassment was looming just around the corner.

As we inaugurated the branch, Gelenski and several other local businesspeople arrived to open their accounts with us. The atmosphere was electric, and I couldn't believe that I was part of such an exciting venture. Working at a bank seemed like a dream come true, and my entire family was overjoyed at my achievement.

We had a formal opening ceremony, with a ribbon-cutting and a cocktail party in the afternoon. I didn't know that the CEO of the bank was going to be there, and I didn't even know who he was. This elegant but obnoxious man, dressed in what seemed to be a very expensive suit, came in and without introducing himself, asked me when I was going home to put on a beautiful dress. I didn't know what to say. I didn't have a party dress, and I didn't know who to call to borrow one. I was so embarrassed that I turned pale in seconds, and my thoughts started racing, *"If this man only knew where I lived, if he only knew how hard it was for me to get this outfit.*" The man didn't back down. I wanted to shout, "*I don't have on*e."

My manager witnessed the situation. Although he did not know me, he could see that I didn't have a dress and was unsure about what to do. He approached me and said, "Let's go for a ride into town." We then headed to my godmother's house, which was only five minutes away from the bank.

I put up my hair, applied some makeup, went back to the car, and said, "I'm really sorry, but I couldn't find a dress that fits me."

He said, "No worries. I just wanted him to forget about the dress."

We went back to the bank, and the man ignored me for the rest of the day. He left without me knowing his name.

While working at the bank, I was able to save money to help my father build a better house for our family. The new house was modest, with a bedroom for my parents and two additional bedrooms for me and my siblings. For the first time, we had a "bathroom" in our home. It was a small space where my father ingeniously hung up a bucket with the shower attachment on it. The bucket was filled with water that we heated on the woodstove, allowing us to enjoy warm showers every day. There was still no toilet as no indoor plumbing existed and no electricity in the house yet, but at least we had a proper place for personal hygiene, and privacy.

I enjoyed working at the bank, but I wanted to explore other options and learn new skills for personal and professional growth. I left Bamerindus and took an internship at Banco do Brasil. This allowed me to earn more money and continue supporting my family. In order to become a full-time employee at Banco do Brasil, I needed to pass a national test, which the bank only administered when there was a need for new employees. Sometimes, people had to wait for years after taking the test to be hired. However, I knew that they hired students, so as long as I was in school, I would have a job. Plus, the salary was much better than what I earned as an employee at Bamerindus.

I knew my employment at Banco do Brasil was only temporary, but my main concern was to support my family financially. I was discontented with my boss at Bamerindus, who had assigned me to work solo at the Fazenda Rio Grande branch. This meant I had to take the bus and transport all the money deposited for the day, which was an extremely perilous task. I was constantly anxious about the potential dangers of being targeted for robbery or kidnapping during these journeys. Even though I was just a teenager at the time, I was acutely aware of the responsibility I shouldered, and I was determined not to prolong this risky situation.

I thoroughly enjoyed working at Banco do Brasil. The atmosphere was pleasant and we were well-compensated. We also received great benefits, which kept everyone in good spirits. I worked alongside Jiocondo, Beth, and Stan at the Agudos do Sul branch, which was approximately twenty-seven kilometers from Mandirituba. Every day, we would meet at 9:00 a.m. in Mandirituba before traveling together to Agudos do Sul. Our branch primarily handled loans for farmers in the region. Although I was eager to be productive, there wasn't always much to do, so I spent a lot of time reading manuals to familiarize myself with the bank's policies and procedures. Of course, I also chatted with my colleagues about current events. During lunch breaks, we often visited a lovely restaurant called Churrascaria Serrana, where we indulged in the traditional Brazilian rodizio. The servers would bring various high-quality cuts of meat, pork, chicken, and sometimes exotic meats like javalí (wild pig), all accompanied by fried bananas, collard greens, black beans, and rice.

When my school year came to an end, it was a really tough time to bid farewell, as I had to say goodbye to my job at Banco do Brasil, which was quite emotional for me.

A new challenge would arrive when I was hired to work at the city hall of Mandirituba. I had never been involved with politics. I knew very little about it, but my employment at the city hall brought me close to the insanity and corruption of those elected to serve who use their power for their benefit. I was hired to work in the finance department. I have had no complaints about my bosses except their lack of commitment to work. My first boss, who I will call Luis here, was good-looking, black-haired, skinny, and smoked at least three packs of cigarettes a day. Every time I opened his office door, a cloud of smoke would come out, and my clothes and hair would have that awful smell for the rest of the day. My second boss, who I will call Marin, was a character. He was an early bird, a tall Italian man dressed up for a party and arrived to work every day with his hair still wet. The fact that he arrived early didn't mean he stayed at work. I was always left with problems to solve, which I had no authority over, while he spent time with his mistress in the afternoon. I could go on and on about this place, but I'd rather say that even though politics are corrupt, people who work for them or at certain institutions are not.

University

The movement of the wheels over the highway and the brassy sound of the motor as the bus stopped and accelerated again, following straight lines and curves, each angled in its awkward way, bothered me. The old seats and windows shook with every tiny bump in the roadway, knocking the riders back and forth. For about two hours from the small town of Mandirituba to the large city of Curitiba, I sometimes took four bus rides among strangers who chattered and laughed loudly.

The final bus ride was about fifteen minutes from the center of Curitiba to my college campus, shared with many students who, like myself, were taking evening classes. Due to better road conditions in the city, that ride seemed to go by faster without a single bump. As the bus arrived at Pontificia Universidade Catolica de Paraná, the driver called, "Catolica stop." I got off the bus and started my journey to a long evening in the classroom.

Though I was a farmer's daughter, I was attending a very prestigious Catholic university. I was again experiencing the cultural shock between the rich and the poor, the city and the rural area. My classmates were all women, many already working as secretaries for international companies, who would arrive straight from their offices wearing fancy, expensive clothes, shoes, and purses. It seemed like a fashion show. I, on the other hand, wore a pair of jeans, sneakers, and a T-shirt. I never wanted to embarrass them with my not-so-fancy clothes, so I opted to sit in the back of the classroom. I always believed that bright students sat in the back of the class, not in the front seats, and my clothes didn't lessen who I was. I was never bitter.

I admired their style and hoped that one day, I would be as successful as they were and would also wear Arezzo, Coach, and Louis Vuitton.

I didn't belong to the group; however, I had passed all the math, English, chemistry, physics, and Portuguese exams required to be accepted to the university. I reminded myself of this often and never diminished myself because I wasn't well dressed like them. I believed that we were all there for a higher education, so regardless of background or circumstances, we could all learn and debate different subjects at the same level intellectually. While my classmates went to the cafeteria and purchased a good meal before class, I would buy only a bag of popcorn from the cart at the university gate that cost fifty cents. I would eat half before class and save the other half to enjoy during my bus rides back home.

The popcorn salesman, Mr. G, was a polite, gracious gentleman who worked honestly to provide for his family. His frail face displayed suffering. Mr. G. knew all the students hanging out around his popcorn cart. He mentioned that he had once dreamed of attending this same univeristy, but his dream would remain only a dream. Yet his enthusiasm for others never wavered. As he sold each popcorn bag, he encouraged the students. "Do good, kids. Make your parents proud." Those words were pronounced as if each student was one of his own. We were all his children and see Mr. G every evening for four years. His charismatic speech and wishes for success to everyone were as constant as the delicious taste and the smell of popcorn with bacon. You may ask, "Popcorn with bacon?" Yes, popcorn with bacon!

My father was brought to mind whenever Mr. G wished me good luck. He dreamed that one day, at least one of his children would become a college graduate. In Brazil, the best universities are federal institutions, but because they are free, the competition is much stiffer than that of private universities. Students who pass the tests usually do not need to work and have time to prepare for them. To have access to free education, one must be intelligent or wealthy.

In 1993, three years after graduating from high school, I boldly decided to apply for college with no money from my parents to finance it. I was blessed with two amazing identical twin friends,

THE DIRT ROAD

Elaine and Eliane (even their names spelled almost the same), who were geniuses by nature and wealthy by birth. They were born in a traditional family that owned many properties and two supermarkets in Mandirituba. They knew my desire to go to college, and as they were taking extra classes to prepare for the exams, three months before the tests, I would go to their house every evening to study their material. They were kind enough to teach me whatever they learned that day. I spent hours with them. Sometimes, I would sleep over at their house so we could spend more time studying. Even though I had been out of school for only three years, the subjects were complex. But Elaine, especially, always made sure that I understood it, and if I didn't, she would patiently explain it again until she was confident that I had learned. I will be forever grateful for such gestures.

In January 1994, about ten kids from Mandirituba had taken the tests, and amazingly, only Elaine, Eliane, and I passed. As I celebrated the excitement of that moment, I felt a deep sadness. I was making about $49 a month, and the cost of tuition was $51 monthly. At that time, I was working for an accounting company, and my boss, Mr. Cesar N., was caring enough to pay my salary in advance so I could enroll in the classes. The university had a policy that if you paid the first month, you could attend classes for six months; before reenrolling for the next six months, you would have to settle the debt to continue taking classes. My parents had taught my siblings and me to avoid owing money and never take advantage of the system. We were taught to give a hand, not take a hand out. The idea that I was somehow taking advantage of the system was not a good feeling.

Since it was a Catholic university, I often attended mass before class. The mass was short to allow the students to go to church and arrive at the class on time. I humbly asked God for wisdom, faith, and strength, never to give up no matter what. I knew deep in my heart that I was not alone. God would never abandon me and would guide me through my journey. With faith in my heart and the desire to succeed, I would check the bulletin board in the hallway every other evening for news or anything I could learn from. Most of the time, there was almost nothing interesting, but I would religiously check it every other evening. Just before the six months of tuition was due, when I had no idea what I would do to settle the debt; there was a note on the bulletin board about a scholarship.

I carefully read the requirements. Only one student would qualify for that particular fund. The next day, I gathered all the paperwork and dropped it off at the financial office, hoping that I would be that one student. While waiting for the answer, I kept checking the bulletin board, and two weeks later, a little note read that I had been selected for an 80 percent scholarship going forward. I read my name several times to ensure it was true; my hands trembled, and my heart started brimming with joy and gratitude. My father planted a seed of encouragement in my heart. He never said it would be easy but believed the seed would grow and produce fruit, and in patience and faith, the harvest would come, bringing abundance and fulfillment into my life.

I often had to make the tough decision to either buy popcorn or deprive my stomach of food. My desire to get an education and make a difference for myself, my family, and society was so intense that I knew the barriers I had to overcome—starting with my stomach.

Walking back five kilometers in the dark on the dirt road at one in the morning was not an option for me. My friend Doroti had been my classmate in my morning high school. She was compassionate enough to offer me a place to stay at her house during my first year of college. She never charged me a dime—again, the grace of God in my life.

I never wanted to take advantage of her kindness and love. She was already giving me a place to stay, so packing food from her house to take to work or a snack before class was a bit against my principles. She and her family were already doing enough. When I couldn't afford even the fifty-cent cost of the popcorn, and my stomach was growling, I would concentrate on the smell of the bacon. I would mentally picture a bag of popcorn with bacon in my hands, and the hunger pangs would disappear. It worked many times.

My ride back home from class was intense and sometimes dangerous. Late at night, the bus stations were not necessarily a safe place to be, as many drug addicts and criminals would be walking around looking for their next victim. If all rides went well on schedule, I left around 11:00 p.m. and would arrive at Doroti's house around 12:30 a.m. If I missed one ride, I would not arrive home until around 1:00 a.m.

After a few months of taking the buses, I started sharing a ride with a friend of mine, Simara. She was two years ahead of me and was also taking her classes in the evening. I would share the ride with two other friends, Joel and Mara. Even though it was comfortable, it was expensive to share gas and tires, and often, I had to choose—either spending money to buy a sandwich or saving the money to pay for the ride, and I saved for it.

My older sister, Diolete, sponsored me once in a while by giving me $3 for a meal at the cafeteria. Since the day I told her that the cafeteria sold this potato bread filled with catupiri cheese—a soft, mild cheese—she was determined to help me enjoy that extravagance once in a while. I felt in paradise every time I ate that soft, tasty bread, and I will be eternally grateful to my sister for such a kind and generous gesture.

My husband loves popcorn, and every time he makes it, the smell of it brings me back to those nights when popcorn was all I ate to survive.

I don't enjoy it anymore.

Even after being granted the scholarship, I constantly looked at the bulletin board. I was hungry for knowledge and something more for my life. Years earlier, I had left the farm determined to make a difference for myself and others. I saw a note that Siemens Telecommunications was offering an internship to a student, and I applied. I was hired to work four hours to assist the secretary. I would work in the afternoon and then attend classes in the evening.

It was an exceptional opportunity to work for an international company. I worked with a secretary named Elisabeth K., who taught me what I needed professionally and in life. Since I only worked four hours, the money I made was not enough for my expenses. I again started looking for more work and soon found the best job I ever had. The only inconvenience was that I had to be at work at seven in the morning. It meant that I only slept four hours between the time

I got home from college and the time I had to get up to take the bus at 5:45 a.m. and get to work by 7:00 a.m.

I got a job at a prestigious tech school in Curitiba called CEFET. My only job was to hoist the flag in the morning, where I learned all the protocols with the flag, from folding it to saluting the flag and wearing white gloves to hold the flag. Then I would go to the cafeteria, bring two thermoses of coffee to the teachers, and eventually, talk to the students if they needed something. I "worked" from 7:00 a.m. to 12:00 noon, walked about ten minutes to Siemens Telecommunications, and worked from 1:00 p.m. to 5:00 p.m. My classes started at 7:00 p.m. I often walked about an hour to my university to save the bus fare. Finance was a complicated subject for me. I had no money growing up. When I started making money, I always struggled to save it regardless of where I worked or how much I made. I had no understanding of how to save it. I had this poor mentality to survive for the day without thinking much about the future regarding finance.

To make matters worse, a well-intentioned friend introduced me to a loan shark as a potential solution to my financial needs. In desperation to clear my debts, I naively placed my trust in the notion that such a person could offer assistance. I was introduced to this nice woman who lent me the money, and for a short time, it felt great to have money and pay my debts. However, the interest rate was so high that I often could not make any payment amount toward the principal. I sometimes had to use most of my monthly meal vouchers to cover the interest, leaving me with no money or vouchers for meals. In Brazil, many companies provide their employees with salary, meal vouchers, and transportation fare as components of their employment benefits package. It was a struggle for me for a long time, but I repaid all my debts and gained a valuable lesson: seemingly effortless choices can turn into arduous challenges. I have learned not to make hasty decisions out of desperation, as they can have hostile consequences.

My financial situation was dire to the point where I would not participate in my graduation celebrations due to my inability to cover the required monthly fee. As always, some kind hearted souls lent me a helping hand in my time of need; two of my classmates, Sandra and Lizi, understanding my financial constraints, took action, organizing a raffle to fund my graduation celebration and ensuring I could join the festivities with them. Sandra and Lizi faced criticism for their actions, yet they proceeded unwaveringly. Their intentions were pure, and they sought no approval from anyone. God knew their hearts, and no applause was necessary. I have not been able to fully repay Sandra and Lizi's act of love, but I have continued to pay forward in their honor over the years.

My graduation remains one of the most amazing moments of my life. It was a joyous occasion, and my parents, siblings, friends, and godmother Marta were present to witness the ceremony. I will forever cherish the moment the ceremonialist invited us to locate our parents amid the crowd; as I descended from the stage, I saw my father, who was the first to rise eagerly, ready to embrace me. That night, my father beamed with pride, and I will carry the memory of that moment with me for the rest of my life.

I was in my third year of college and was hired as an employee at Siemens Telecommunications. I had moved to Curitiba and shared an apartment with a friend. It was the beginning of enormous changes in my life. At Siemens, I had the opportunity to develop new skills. I started as an intern and learned everything in the training department.

My department was in charge of the infrastructure for different telecommunication technique classes in Brazil and worldwide. When a client brought new telecommunication equipment, the training department was responsible for setting up theoretical and practical courses, supplies, and certifications. All that was necessary for the engineers to teach the telecommunication system, implement industrial communication networks, and connect them to an enterprise network, which demanded a great deal of ability and accessible specialist knowledge. A team of engineers was well-trained to teach the telecommunications system and how it was operated, planned, designed, maintained, and the security needed to diagnose a problem. Siemens developed a training program and subsequent certification aligned with international industrial standards. Each certificate documented that the client had enough skills as part of the overall Siemens industrial training program and could operate Siemens telecommunications equipment.

After I graduated from college, I enrolled in an MBA program at Universidade Positivo. A master's degree program was expensive, but I could handle it. I had been in financial difficulties before. I planned to move to a new apartment to save on the rent. The head boss of my department had heard that I was enrolled in the MBA program and called me in for a meeting. At first, I was concerned when the big boss called me in. I didn't know what to think, but I went to the meeting confident that whatever it was, I would handle it professionally. To my surprise, he said I was just awarded full tuition from Siemens Telecommunications for my MBA program. At that moment, I had no words to express my gratitude. I thought of my father when he helped people fix their cars late at night without charging them and told my mom, "One day, it could be one of my children, and I want them to get help."

America

It was a fresh spring morning when I landed on foreign soil. I had been on an eleven-hour flight from Sao Paulo, Brazil, to Newark, New Jersey, international airport. The plane landed, and the pilot announced that we had arrived in the United States of America. There was a mixture of exhilaration and apprehension as I embarked on a journey of a lifetime, leaving my family, friends, and a great job behind. Standing outside the airport, I couldn't help but reflect on the challenges that would inevitably be waiting for me in the new land I would call home for a while.

Leaving Brazil was hard, especially leaving my family behind. My father was completely opposed to it. On April 13, 1999, I got up early in the morning to find my father in the kitchen, ready to leave the house; he had a frown face that showed how angry he was at me. I asked him for his blessings. He responded upset and said, "Don't take too long to return; otherwise, you won't find us alive." And with those words, he left the house that morning. I understood his feelings, but I was following my dreams and knew deep in my heart that was precisely what I had to do.

It was springtime in 1999 when I arrived in the United States with $600 in my pocket and the courage to deal with the unknown. I spoke no English, but my goal was to learn English and return to Brazil within a year.

I had been to Disney World, Florida, the year before and didn't like it, and the idea of moving to the United States of America was not in my plans, but I could do it for a year because I was motivated to learn and speak English fluently. Doing so would bring personal growth, better opportunities, and a deep connection with the world. Initially, it felt like an exhilarating adventure tinged with a touch of fear.

Since I could not afford school and was trying to figure out what to do, I started going to the park with my notebook and dictionary, hoping to meet someone there willing to help me with English. I was living with my friend Sandra and her family. Sandra and I had met in Brazil years earlier when we both taught first graders. We were at my apartment in Curitiba when we decided to come to the United States. Sandra's husband was already here, so she was coming with her daughter, Gabriela, to reunite the family, and I would come to learn the language. I traveled a month later after making sure all my affairs in Brazil were taken care of.

I spent hours in the park listening to people talk and trying to learn new words from their conversations, but I couldn't. I was determined to learn the language and knew the sacrifice I was making. I had just finished my MBA and had given up a great job in Brazil. I was fully aware of the road ahead of me.

I kept going to the park. One beautiful afternoon, I saw an attractive guy walking around and looking curious. I thought he wanted to talk to me, but without any English skills, how could I begin a conversation? That afternoon, I came back home frustrated. The next day, both of us were in the park again, and suddenly, he came up and asked my name and where I was from. I barely understood the questions, but I was able to respond. I asked his name, and he said, "Michael." He was very handsome in his early twenties, had the most gorgeous blue eyes, and wore glasses like those intellectual actors I had seen on TV. My interaction with Michael was through word-for-word translation with the help of my dictionary. Michael looked confused but understood we would meet again at the park the next day.

The day was absolutely breathtaking. As we reunited in the afternoon, I couldn't help but notice that the sky mirrored the shade of blue in Michael's eyes. Michael was from Minnesota and had come to New Jersey to attend law school. I asked him if he could teach me some English, and without hesitation, he said, "Yes." That was incredibly generous of him. He became my tutor and spent hours with me daily while waiting for his classes to start. Sometimes, our communication was through pictures and drawings in my notebook, but it was delightful. Michael's patience, kindness, and understanding were crucial in aiding the development of my English skills.

Michael was the first person who introduced me to American culture. He took me to a pizzeria, and it was the first time I ate pizza without a fork and knife like we do in Brazil. He took me to the movies and shopping. I can only imagine his frustration trying to communicate with me, and many times I could not form a sentence to start a conversation. He also filed all the paperwork necessary to extend my stay in the United States of America. I had a ten-year visa, but when you enter the United States, you are granted six months to stay as a tourist. I was granted permission to stay, but I never got to inform him about it. Our goodbyes were already said, and his university classes had begun, preventing him from teaching me further. Unfortunately, I never crossed paths with him again. I am forever thankful to Michael for his kind gesture, which he didn't have to do but did so anyway. Wherever he may be, I wish him happiness, good health, and success in his career as an attorney at law.

As an immigrant, one often has to do whatever it takes to make a living and thrive in a new country. I remember one afternoon when Sandra and I went to a car wash near our house, and we saw a note that said, "Help Wanted". They needed someone to dry the cars. Since they all spoke Spanish, I was able to communicate with them and was hired to start the next day.

The job started off as a source of enjoyment for me. Instead of focusing on improving my English skills, I found myself improving my Spanish language abilities. Having studied Spanish for four years at the university, this job provided the perfect opportunity to practice my language skills. The employees at the car wash hailed from various countries in South and Central America, each with a unique and compelling story about their journey to the United States. Some had left loved ones, including wives and children, behind. Others, much like myself, had abandoned promising careers. This experience reinforced the idea that as human beings, we often pass judgment on others without truly understanding their life stories. It became evident that some people endure immense hardships but wear a brave smile every day, while others blessed with comfortable lives wake up with resentment towards the world. This exposure to different life experiences taught me that everyone has their own struggles and victories. The summer of 1999 in Kearny, New Jersey provided the perfect opportunity to interact and learn from the diverse individuals at the car wash. The remarkable men at the car wash imparted powerful lessons of empathy, encouraging me to actively listen and understand others - a lesson that remains etched in my memory.

On a scorching day, my coworkers were unexpectedly absent from work, I found myself alone in the sweltering heat at the car wash. I worked tirelessly in the shimmering heat, meticulously tending to each vehicle that passed through. The relentless stream of cars seemed unceasing as I carefully dried them and delicately applied shining oil to their tires. Despite feeling frustrated and tempted to give up, I reminded myself of my determination not to quit. As an MBA graduate in the United States learning the language, I recognized the importance of persisting towards my goal, and I refused to let the challenging circumstances deter me. Although the day was chaotic and demanding, I persevered by focusing on my long-term aspirations and the significance of the experience for my personal and professional growth.

The next day, I left the frustration behind, smiled, and returned to the car wash to start over. I worked with my colleagues to dry many cars and had a good day.

As the colder months approached, I realized that working at the car wash wouldn't be practical during wintertime. Personally, I've never been a fan of winter, and the thought of dealing with snow was particularly daunting as I had never encountered it before. I recall being paid $5 an hour and receiving decent tips. However, at the conclusion of each day, we were required to combine all our tips and share them with the manager, which often left us with much less than we had earned. Despite this, I still appreciated having cash in my hands at the end of each shift.

THE DIRT ROAD

My friend Sandra's husband worked for a construction company, and his boss needed someone to assist his wife. I was asked if I would like to work as a live-in with the family. I accepted the offer and moved with the family to their breathtaking house in Wayne, New Jersey. Years earlier, I thought the Gelenski's house was a mansion, but now I was in a castle.

Sara and Masoud, originally from Iran, had been living in the United States for many years. They were proud parents of a twelve-year-old son named Ali, who took great delight in my accent as I was still learning English. The way I pronounced words always amused him. Ali's close friend, Tom, was a frequent visitor to their home, and they both derived great joy from listening to my accent. Their laughter and giggles were a delightful and heartwarming soundtrack in the household.

Fluffy, the family's beloved green eyed black cat, would often be found lazily wandering around the house, eagerly awaiting Ali's return from school.

Sara has always been a gorgeous woman with a Middle Eastern look. She had a knack for dressing elegantly, ensuring her shoes matched her purse and her nails complemented her lipstick. Cooking Persian dishes was a passion of hers. We would often spend our evenings preparing zucchini and eggplant. Despite my limited English, I always felt at ease talking with Sara about anything, perhaps because we were both foreigners. She had a unique way of understanding my emotions, whether I was feeling sad or content. Sara and Masoud were known for regularly hosting parties for their friends, so we were frequently in the kitchen preparing food. I enjoyed being Sara's sous-chef, chopping eggplant, cucumbers, tomatoes, and whatever else she needed for her delicious Persian dishes.

In the months leading up to 2000, widespread concern was about the "millennium bug" causing computer and electronic malfunctions. Some people even went as far as to predict the world's end. Amidst this uncertainty, Sara hosted an extravagant party at her house, to which guests traveled from far and wide, including California, New York, and New Jersey. I vividly remember wearing a stunning black gown and a silver tiara to welcome the New Year in style. The relief we all felt was palpable when the clock struck midnight, and nothing catastrophic happened.

During that period, I fully devoted myself to my English studies and diligently attended English classes in the evenings at a language school twice a week in Kearny, NJ. The journey involved taking multiple buses from Wayne to the Willowbrook Mall, then from the mall to Newark, and finally from Newark to Kearny, rain or shine. After class, I would stay at Sandra's house and return by the same route the following day. On Friday afternoons, I eagerly looked forward to being picked up by Sandra, knowing I would spend a delightful weekend with her family. I intended to stay in the United States for a year, learn English, return home, and find a job at an international company; more specifically, I dreamed of working for Volvo. The breathtaking city of Curitiba, with its winding streets and vibrant culture, had never seen me set foot in a Volvo showroom, much less behind the wheel of a Volvo car. Yet, it was my fervent desire to one day be employed by Volvo and make Brazil my forever home. As fate would have it, that was my personal plan, but evidently, it was not in alignment with God's plan.

One morning, I woke up with excruciating pain on my left side, a pain that I had never felt before. Sara took me to a gynecologist, Dr. K. Behnam, who was also from Iran. Dr. Behnam ordered an ultrasound, and the next day, I was taken to the OR for the removal of an ovarian cyst. I remember Dr. Behnam asking me before the procedure,

"Do you know why you are here?"

With my broken English, I responded, "I am here for surgery."

Then, in seconds, the anesthesia took over my body, and I remember waking up in the hospital with Sara by my side with a note written on a napkin, a note that I still have.

"Dear Janete, I've been here with you…and I've taken pictures and talked to Dr. Behnam…everything is fine. I'll be going to pick up Ali after school I will be back to see you here again. Don't worry, just rest. Okay. Everybody here is nice. (I have a little gift for you, open it.)

Love, Sara."

THE DIRT ROAD

Now, my one-year plan took an unexpected turn; my primary focus shifted to generating income. I needed to pay Dr. Behnam, who had graciously performed my surgery and was patiently waiting for compensation.

After the surgery, I couldn't work for a week, and I had to go back to Sandra's house. Sandra was so kind and took care of me, even helping me with things like giving me a shower when I couldn't do it myself during my post-op recovery.

At my next doctor's visit, I met Dr. Behnam's wife, and during our conversation, she inquired about my occupation. I mentioned that I was currently employed by Sara. Mrs. Behnam expressed her need for assistance, which led me to discuss the opportunity with Sara. Following our conversation, I agreed to assist Mrs. Behnam with household chores on Mondays. Since both Sara's and Mrs. Behnam's houses were not easily accessible, Sara kindly offered to drive me to a convenient meeting point where Mrs. Behnam would then pick me up. Then, in the afternoon, it was Mrs. Behnam's turn to drop me off at the meeting point, and Sara would pick me up. On the journey, I appreciated the lovely scenery.

Despite the initial language barrier, we gradually began to communicate and engage in meaningful conversation about English classes, my family back home, and, more importantly, my higher education in Brazil. Mrs. Behnam was grateful for my assistance which filled me with satisfaction and a sense of fulfillment.

After undergoing surgery, I found myself in a tough spot when Sandra's husband let me know that they could no longer accommodate my weekend stay at their house. I was uncertain about where to go, so I reached out to my friend Silvio. Thankfully, he and his brother kindly offered me a place to stay for the weekend while I sorted out my living arrangements.

I remember Silvio and I meeting in our English classes and quickly becoming great friends. We used to spend much time studying in the classroom and sometimes even met on weekends to practice our English-speaking skills. However, I didn't get along with his brother. Even though his brother never did anything to harm me, I always felt very uncomfortable around him. There was something in his eyes that made me panic. Eventually, I made the tough decision to take a break from school to sort out my living situation. Leaving school was difficult because I was so committed to learning the language. The language school had an excellent English teacher, Virginia O. She wasn't just the owner of the school but also a brilliant, charismatic, and empathetic woman who fluently spoke eight languages. Virginia was a naturally talented English teacher, and I consider myself extremely fortunate to have had her as my teacher. I owe her tremendous gratitude for teaching me the language and giving me a job at her language school after graduation.

Sara and Massod sold their beloved home to the Renjen family, a wonderful Indian family with two adorable children named Poonya and Kushal. As they worked through the selling process, I had the opportunity to interact with the Renjen family often, and over time, we developed a close friendship.

After relocating to Sara's new house, I was immediately struck by the grandeur of our breathtaking new home. The high ceilings seemed to reach for the sky, while the expansive rooms provided ample space to roam. The kitchen was a vision of modern elegance, with its sleek design and top-of-the-line appliances. As I crossed the threshold, I felt as though I had entered a realm of luxury fit for royalty. Situated atop a mountain, the house offered sweeping panoramic views of Wayne, NJ, allowing us to bask in the grandeur of nature from the comfort of our own home.

A week later, Sara left the house with her cousin for a meeting, and her husband told me he was bringing me to see their new office, which was about half a mile away. I didn't think anything extraordinary because, from what I understood, the Verizon technician was going to be there, which he was. I never did anything without calling Sara first, but that day, I don't know why, I didn't call her. Nevertheless, I thought I would go there, see the office, return home, and continue my work duties. Sara got home to find me missing. She drove to the office, furious at her husband and me. They engaged in a heated confrontation in their native language. I had no idea what was happening, and it was distressing. I never did anything wrong and would never hurt Sara. She had been incredibly gracious to me all those months I was at their house. She told me that she could no longer trust me. Disheartened, I left her house for good that afternoon. I loved her and could not comprehend what had just happened.

With no place to go, I went back to school, not knowing where I would sleep that night. I had been poor, but I always had a roof over my head, and I was now homeless. At school, I told my friend Elizabeth what had happened and that I did not know where to go. Elizabeth and I crossed paths at the language school. She struck me as a beautiful person with a truly kind heart, always prepared to lend a helping hand to those in need. That particular night, I found myself seeking her assistance. She called a friend who had a place for me to stay. The room was in the unfinished basement where the plumbing room was. There was no bed, so I slept on the floor with the sound of water passing through the plumbing system all night long; that was what they had to offer, and I, on the other hand, had no option but to accept it.

I was starting all over again. I hated myself for being in the United States. I again badly wanted to go back home, and I started looking for jobs in Brazil, but all the positions I found required English fluency. I could not take the chance of embarrassing myself and others with my English skills, so I decided to stay and try again. I got a job with a cleaning company where we cleaned seven houses daily. I left at 6:00 a.m. and came back at 6:30 p.m. I always ran around to get to my English class at 7:00 p.m., but I would not miss one. On the weekends, I would babysit to earn more money to move to a better place. Soon after, my friend Rose got me a job as a waitress at a country club on the weekends. We usually worked between three to four parties per weekend, including weddings, bar mitzvahs, and birthday parties. The Spanish I had practiced at the car wash months earlier was now in good use with my new coworkers at the country club.

Rose is an extraordinary woman! Her constant smile and achievements are a testament to her exceptional character. She immigrated from Brazil, learned English, and was already in her late forties when she went to college for the first time in America and became a social worker. It was delightful to work with Rose at the country club. Her contagious sense of humor made the challenging moments more enjoyable. We would often finish working at 11:30 p.m. and then go to the movies for a midnight show, knowing that at 8:00 a.m., we would have to be back at work. I am grateful to Rose for her friendship and companionship and for finding me that job when I needed it the most.

Even though the room was a contrast from Sara's castle and I was unfamiliar with Elizabeth's friend, they warmly welcomed me into their home, and I respectfully addressed them as Aunt Tide and Uncle GP. Uncle GP has departed from us, now residing in heaven, and his absence is deeply felt as I hold fond memories of him. I have a deep affection for Aunt Tide. She is a talented artist whose paintings are marvelous, and her humor always makes me laugh. Aunt Tide is always available to talk and lend a listening ear. Her unwavering support and dependable shoulder to lean on are invaluable in times of need, and she has been a pillar of strength for me. It's reassuring to know that Aunt Tide is only a phone call away whenever I need her advice. Hearing her voice brings me comfort and familiarity, just like a mother's presence. I cherish the bond I share with her, and it's a unique and meaningful relationship. Their house was always filled with the sound of laughter and music on Sundays. The air was rich with the aromas of delicious Brazilian food, creating an atmosphere of warmth and comfort. It was more than just a place; it was a space where joy, friendship, and love intertwined, forming the essence of a home that I find myself yearning for time and time again. In their home, I met remarkable individuals who have become essential to my life's journey. One of them is Rosinha, she holds a significant place in my heart as an incredibly important and cherished friend. I deeply value her reliability, as she is always there when I need her. Moreover, her wonderful sense of humor never fails to brighten our conversations and fill them with joy. Their two daughters, Ana Paula and Nilde, are both amazing women: loving mothers, devoted wives, and cherished friends who I admire and love with all my heart.

Eventually, I moved in with Lilly, Roger, and Carlos. Lilly and Roger were dating, and I barely saw them due to our work schedules. Carlos and I became good friends because we were both from South

Brazil. We connected and were each other's confidants. Carlos was passionate about pursuing a career as an airplane pilot, but ultimately chose to prioritize his marriage instead.

When Lilly and Roger broke up. Lilly and I needed a new roommate to share the household expenses. My friend Alyne was my classmate back in college and had moved to the United States. I contacted her and asked if she would like to share the house, and to my surprise, she said yes. She moved in, and Lilly and Alyne instantly bonded, forming a strong and enduring friendship. Lilly was younger than us, possessed a captivating charm, spoke English with almost no accent, and had a delightful sense of humor.

I have never been much of a night person. I prefer staying home reading a book or trying new recipes, so I wasn't the ideal companion for their vibrant nightlife adventures. They both shared a deep enthusiasm for the nocturnal scene and frequently shared stories with me, and we all had a blast! I deeply admired the beauty of their friendship. Occasionally, I would go on a date, and they both joyfully celebrated such an achievement. I frequently recall the days when we shared the house, and I speculate how different things would be if those times were today.

After years had passed and our paths diverged, Alyne and I found ourselves reconnecting and sharing a deep and meaningful friendship. Amidst the changes we both have undergone, we unearthed a multitude of shared interests that have further strengthened our bond. I've always admired Alyne's work ethic and unwavering honesty.

The Opportunity

After leaving Sara's house, I continued to work for Mrs. Behnam. My journey to Mrs. Behnam's house was quite an adventure. I would take the bus from Kearny to Newark, then another bus to the Willowbrook Mall in Wayne, and then Mrs. Behnam would kindly pick me up at a specific bus stop in Wayne. I was determined to learn English, so while eagerly waiting for Mrs. Behnam, I would sit on the curb, open my book, and diligently do my homework. As my English proficiency improved and I became more adept in communication, I took the opportunity to share my educational background with Mrs. Behnam and explain the reasons for my relocation to the United States.

After missing out on a job opportunity at Siemens Telecommunication in Brazil due to a lack of English skills, I made the decision to leave the country and pursue my goals in the United States. Despite only knowing basic phrases like "hi," "bye," and "thank you," I was determined not to let language barriers hinder my opportunities again. I had attempted to take classes in Brazil, but attending school only once a week without daily practice proved to be ineffective for me. This experience drove me to fully commit to learning English and ensuring that language would never hold me back from seizing opportunities in the future.

Mrs. Behnam played a motherly role in my life. She was always there to advise me, whether I was feeling homesick or had questions about anything. I frequently turned to her for comfort and guidance. She strongly believed that the United States provided great opportunities for me if I worked hard and learned the language, and she genuinely trusted in my abilities to do more and better. Whenever I considered returning home, she gave me many compelling reasons to stay. I was torn between believing her and my own doubts, and this internal conflict lasted a long time. Mrs. Behnam graciously welcomed me into her home and her heart; her consistent support, trust, guidance, and belief in my potential are things that I deeply treasure. Throughout the years, I have expressed gratitude to her for being an incredible presence in my life. Yet, she humbly deflects the praise, insisting that anyone else would have done the same, though I remain unconvinced.

One quiet Sunday afternoon, I was enjoying the company of my roommates, Alyne and Lilly, when the unexpected sound of the house phone cut through the tranquility. To my surprise, it was Dr. Behnam on the line, expressing Mrs. Behnam's confidence in my potential to work in their office. They believed that my proficient English skills made me an ideal fit for the front desk and patient aid position, offering me the opportunity to learn new skills in the medical field. Without inquiring about the compensation, I eagerly accepted the offer, feeling like I was graduating from household chores to a professional office role. Dr. Behnam then informed me that they expected me to commence work at 9 am the following day, and I eagerly embraced the prospect of starting my new job so soon. Months before this exciting turn of events, Mrs. Behnam had been diligently handling the paperwork with the immigration department to change my status in the United States, and I was filled with anxious anticipation for the forthcoming outcome.

I had never worked in a doctor's office before, and working directly with people is not my strongest skill. I prefer working with computers, numbers, and papers. To my surprise, Dr. Behnam's patients were the best. They were kind and always understood when I could not pronounce a medical term properly. I had learned with Nene years earlier the gift of being compassionate, and once again, I was practicing kindness, patience, and understanding with all the patients who arrived at the office and then were diagnosed with cancer. Some of them I would see often and some of them would be gone too soon.

I had the incredible opportunity to work alongside Dr. K. Behnam, and it has truly been the most rewarding and fulfilling experience of my professional career. As my immediate supervisor, Dr. K. Behnam consistently demonstrated an unwavering dedication to the well-being of his patients as well as to myself. His approach to patient care was characterized by profound respect, genuine care, and deep compassion for each individual.

In his role as an oncologist gynecologist, Dr. K. Behnam exhibited an exceptional level of expertise and provided the highest standard of care to every woman who sought his medical guidance. What set him apart was his ability to communicate the full reality of a severe diagnosis to his patients with a rare blend of honesty and empathy, ensuring that they felt informed and supported without unnecessary fear or discomfort.

Dr. K. Behnam was truly adored by all his patients, who saw him as their doctor and healer. I have personally witnessed countless women coming into his office feeling anxious and unsettled about their diagnoses, only to leave after talking with Dr. K. Behnam with an overwhelming sense of peace and confidence in their treatment plan. Dr. K. Behnam had this incredible ability to remember his patients and their diagnoses even after years without seeing them. Sometimes, he would call me in the evening and ask about a new patient whose name he had forgotten. I would mention just one word about what I remember about the patient. Sometimes, all I had to say was the name of the physician who referred the patient to him, and he would remember everything about that patient. He always made each patient a priority, showing his true commitment, and dedication to their well-being by ensuring he returned every single phone call and addressed all of their concerns.

After office hours, Dr. K. Behnam and I would sit down together to review the day's cases and assign the appropriate codes for insurance billing. Dr. K. Behnam not only taught me accurate procedural coding and diagnosis but also had a passion for using visual aids. He often sketched pictures to illustrate each procedure code. Under his guidance, I gained invaluable practical knowledge that I couldn't have acquired in a traditional classroom setting.

THE DIRT ROAD

Whenever I assisted Dr. K. Behnam or responded to his inquiries, he would affectionately say, "Janet, what would I do without you?"

To which I consistently replied, "Many things, Dr. Behnam."

As I started my new role, I was quickly entrusted with overseeing office operations after the office manager underwent surgery. Despite my initial lack of knowledge about running a doctor's office, I embraced the challenge confidently and embarked on a journey to acquire the skills necessary to handle surgical scheduling and manage extensive communication with hospitals, patients, and insurance companies.

One afternoon at the office, Mrs. Behnam, approached me with a question: "Do you know what an EOB is?" I had to admit that I didn't. She patiently explained that it stood for "Explanation of Benefits." Intrigued by this aspect of the insurance industry, I made the decision to pursue further education. I enrolled in a comprehensive medical assistant program at William Paterson University. This step marked a significant personal challenge as I stretched my academic horizons into new territories. The course was intellectually stimulating, and I eagerly absorbed the knowledge. However, as the curriculum progressed to include practical lab sessions, my unease with needles became a significant obstacle. Recognizing this, I recalibrated my academic focus toward medical billing, a field that allowed me to leverage my growing expertise without confronting this particular fear.

I had the opportunity to collaborate with Doris, whom I had initially met at Dr. Behnam's office. Doris excelled in managing billing and operated her own billing company. I dedicated my days off and vacation time to working with her to familiarize myself with the codes. After completing the billing program, I handled the billing process independently at Dr. Behnam's office. I was nicknamed "good egg" by Doris because I had learned it quickly and without making any notes; it was fresh in my memory. It became evident that I had discovered a genuine passion for working with the codes. Given my long-standing fascination with numbers and finance, delving into medical billing was naturally just right for me. Unlike many peers, I breezed through math during my school years.

Growing up in a small rural community, I always had an entrepreneurial spirit. I knew I didn't want to be a farmer for the rest of my life. I dreamed of working in an office and often pictured my desk, the telephone, eyeglasses, and smoking a cigarette between breaks. The desire to smoke cigarettes has been gone since I left the farm.

When I was in fifth grade, I went to my school's principal's office and asked Dona Joana if she would like to buy sweet potatoes from me. I told her I didn't have any, but I would bring her some the following day. I told Dona Joana that the sweet potatoes from our farm were the best in the region, and we had both white and red sweet potatoes. I assured her that if she bought sweet potatoes from me, she would eat the most delicious sweet potatoes ever. "Also, we don't use pesticides on our farm," I said. Dona Joana listened carefully to my sales pitch and ordered two kilos of sweet potatoes without asking any questions. I would walk those five kilometers my entire fifth-grade year carrying sweet potatoes for Dona Joana.

I had the privilege of meeting the Renjen family when they purchased Sara's previous house. As we became acquainted, they kindly offered me a job doing the household chores at their place. The Renjen family, Indian immigrants, had faced the typical challenges experienced by immigrants on their journey to success. Whenever I was at their house, Mr. Renjen would share bits of his life story, detailing his journey to America, his hard work in a Spanish restaurant, and his eventual rise to CEO of an American company. His words of encouragement and resilience inadvertently became a source of inspiration for me. I was genuinely moved when I saw him being picked up by a chauffeur, looking impeccable in his tailored suit. "*One day, I will be a successful businesswoman,*" I told myself silently, feeling determined as I continued with my chores.

Embarking on the exhilarating journey of launching my own business was undeniably daunting, but I tackled it with unwavering determination. Despite moments of self-doubt and uncertainty, I remained resolute in my commitment to face any challenges that came my way. I firmly believe in embracing every experience as a chance to learn and grow. A powerful quote that deeply resonated with me during this journey is: "If I fail, I will learn. If I succeed, I will teach you." This quote has become my guiding light, reinforcing my confidence to embrace both success and failure as invaluable lessons in my entrepreneurial pursuit.

I felt incredibly grateful to have the support of mentors, entrepreneurs, and friends who believed in me and my vision to open my own business. Their encouragement and guidance were instrumental in bolstering my determination and carrying me through challenging times.

In December 2005 I embarked on the challenging journey of starting a medical billing company. After diligently saving up, I was able to acquire the necessary tools including the billing software, a fax machine, and a computer. I was left with just $100 to open a business account. I owe my savings habits to Mrs. Behnam, who mentored me in the art of saving money. During my employment at her residence, she set up a savings account for me and would routinely inquire, when she paid me, if I needed all of the money. If not, she would deposit it into the savings account for me, and if I did, she would promptly hand it over. Mrs. Behnam's constant encouragement and support motivated me to enroll in billing classes, and when I eventually announced my plan to open my own business, she granted me access to the second floor of their office to kickstart my venture. Mrs. Behnam embraced me with affection and consistently went above and beyond to ensure my well-being and happiness, making me feel like her own adopted child.

Doris had become my closest friend. She and her sister Sandy played a role in the documentation part of my business, helping me apply for a tax ID, register the business, and even open a banking account. Having these two terrific friends by my side made me feel empowered, as they helped and supported me in the journey I was about to start.

I now felt empowered, speaking English fluently and officially opening my own business. Doing business in a country where English was not my first language was quite an achievement. I began the process of billing Dr. Mel's first patient to the insurance company. Dr.

Melody Behnam, the daughter of Dr. K. Behnam and Mrs. Behnam, whom I affectionately refer to as Dr. Mel, and she, in turn, calls me a non biological sister, had faith in my ability to handle this task. Over the years, I have demonstrated that I am capable of managing the complexities of dealing with insurance companies.

The soothing care and compassion that Dr. Mel exhibits reflect the influence of her father, Dr. K. Behnam. Her patients hold her in high regard, and she has provided exceptional care to numerous women through the years, assisting in the delivery of many babies. I have always deeply appreciated the professional bond between Dr. Mel and her father, especially when she served as his assistant surgeon in various procedures. Following each procedure, they engaged in detailed discussions about the findings and the care plan, driven by their deep love and compassion for each individual. Their bond as a father-daughter duo is truly inspiring, and I wish there were more partnerships like theirs in the world. I will always be grateful to Dr. Mel for believing in me and being my first client. Her trust and support have given me the confidence to pursue my business endeavors.

The billing process is more complicated than many people realize. It requires knowledge of coding, finance, and even human anatomy. To succeed in this industry, a great team is essential, from the doctor's office front desk to the doctors themselves who complete medical records. Unfortunately, the process often breaks down by the time it reaches the billing stage, and billers must resort to "performing miracles" to get the claims paid. Dealing with insurance companies presents its own challenges; they often find reasons to deny claims, leaving healthcare providers waiting months for compensation. OB-GYN is a specialty that suffers significantly at the hands of insurance companies. Additionally, working with overseas customer service, particularly in India and the Philippines, can be challenging as their employees are often not well-trained to resolve issues. The number of hours spent on the phone is ridiculous, and most of the time, nothing gets resolved; the issues are "escalated," and the insurance company's representatives ask us to call them back in ten days; "here is your reference number for this call." In ten days, a new call is placed, forty-five minutes on hold to find out nothing has been done to resolve the issue! Also, certified mail never arrives, even though we have the post office delivery confirmation receipt. Insurance companies often tend to initially pay healthcare providers for their services; after several months, they may discover that they have processed the claims with "inaccurate" information in their system. As a result, they will then request a refund of the overpaid amount, causing absolute stress for the provider and the billing department. That's the routine every single day!

A year later, Dr. Mel introduced me to Dr. L. Eyerman, an incredibly compassionate young doctor. Meeting Dr. Eyerman was a true blessing. He genuinely cares about my well-being and growth; he has supported my goals and dreams, offered encouragement and constructive feedback, and constantly lifted my spirits with humor. His witty jokes and playful banter make every challenge seem more manageable, even in the most demanding situations, and I feel empowered to strive for success and take on whatever comes my way. He consistently believed in my potential and wanted me to succeed. He has been my best advocate through the years, providing valuable insights and direction in the medical industry and helping me to build up my business and a positive professional reputation, which has opened up new opportunities. He never hesitates to refer my work to other doctors. Our professional relationship is built on mutual respect and trust, and every day, I express profound gratitude to Dr. Eyerman for his remarkable impact on my business and me.

Reflecting on my journey, I often ask myself if I would do it again. Despite the difficulties, uncertainty, and self-doubt, the answer is always the same: I would do it all over again. Starting out alone, I have grown the business and now employ Americans from all backgrounds. When Mrs. Behnam gave me the opportunity, I committed never to disappoint her. My diligent efforts have allowed me to support numerous individuals in need over the years. However, the most gratifying aspect is recognizing my positive impact on lives through the employment opportunities I have generated in my adopted homeland.

Sara

Two days before setting off on my highly anticipated trip to Vienna, I was filled with eager expectations for the upcoming journey, filled with exploration, art appreciation, and cultural immersion. I envisioned the city's streets resonating with the enchanting melodies of classical music as I wandered through Vienna's lively and colorful streets. From the charming cafes to the picturesque shops lining the bustling streets, I imagined myself taking in the sights and sounds of this vibrant city. The air was filled with the alluring fragrance of freshly brewed coffee and delicate pastries, invoking a sense of excitement and wonder as I prepared for my upcoming adventure.

I was with Client A and going through some paperwork when I unexpectedly felt the urge to leave the office and head to Client B. Normally, I finish tasks for one client before meeting another. But on that particular day, something felt different; perhaps it was the excitement of my trip or some other unknown factor. I informed Client A that I would be heading to Client B but assured them I would return promptly to complete the tasks I had started. As I made my way to Client B, I sensed a distinct atmosphere but couldn't pinpoint what made it different. In my thoughts, I kept thinking, *"It must be the trip!"*

Years ago, I met Sara's mother, who lived in Vienna. She was an elegant, gracious, and sophisticated woman with an impeccable posture that commanded attention and respect. Her carefully styled black hair framed a face adorned with wisdom and life experiences. Her attire reflected refined taste and appreciation for timeless style.

After meeting her, my love for Vienna grew. Despite my limited English-speaking skills at the time, I researched the captivating city, and the more I learned, the stronger my desire to experience it became.

When I returned and entered Client A's office, I saw a familiar woman sitting in the doctor's waiting room. Her face immediately caught my eye, carrying the marks of countless shared memories; seeing her brought back memories of laughter and warmth. Her beautiful eyes and black hair, once vibrant, now held stories of sadness and loneliness. As I greeted her, I was filled with emotions, "Sara?" Despite the pain of our past, my love for Sara still lingered like a delicate strand.

She responded, "Yes, I am Sara."

"I am Janete, I said."

We hugged, and tears gently streamed down our faces. It felt like many conflicting emotions and open wounds collided and found a way to heal, revealing the deep warmth of our love for each other. A sweet and genuine smile appeared on our faces, casting a comforting and inviting glow and reminding us of our special bond. We had found each other again, and it was beautiful.

My Brother's Death

Hundreds of trucks lined up on the highway with engines still running, producing a strong smell of exhaust fumes. I had to cover my nose to breathe. It was a dark day with clouds of sadness in the air. If the rain were going to start, it would be dropping tears of anguish. The drivers looked distressed as they exited their trucks and walked silently for a few minutes. Even their footsteps on the highway were soft and light, but the tense silence surrounding them was screaming sorrow. Unaware of where I was or had come from, I quietly walked with the drivers. It was a procession of men and women, young and old, all together on the shoulder of the highway walking North. They were all strangers from all parts of Brazil walking together, not one of them speaking a word. I was also silent but anxious. I wanted to know what had happened, where I was, and how I had arrived there.

The silence was broken when a stranger tapped my shoulders and said, "It's an accident." He then brought me to the front of a truck. There were no trucks or cars damaged and no signs that an accident had occurred, yet dark-red blood had spewed and started dripping and making a pool all around the two bodies covered with manila cardboard in the middle of the highway. "One is your friend," the stranger said, "You are not supposed to know the identity of the other corpse." I was devastated, confused, and in shock. I sat down on the shoulder of the highway, trying to make sense of what I had heard. It seemed like a puzzle that I could not solve. If it was my friend, which friend? I have many friends. And why was I not supposed to know who the other dead person was? The stranger held my hand, walked me away from the scene, and instructed me to attend the funeral of "my friend." I was then brought to the cemetery, where there was a closed casket with my "friend's" body. I still didn't know who the friend was, so I started asking people at the funeral about the person's identity in the casket, but nobody seemed willing to explain anything to me. I was in the middle of hundreds of people attending the funeral alone and with no answer. Some people around me were the truck drivers I had walked with just hours earlier. I could not comprehend anything that was happening.

I woke up shaking and screaming at my bedroom walls as if someone were there to listen and understand what had just happened, but I only had the dark walls of my bedroom surrounding me. I was alone in my misery and despair. I started shouting, "It was in Mandirituba. It was in Mandirituba." It was so vivid and real. I couldn't fall asleep again. If I closed my eyes, I would see everything all over again. I needed a peaceful night's sleep, but it was impossible. My hands were sweating, my heart was accelerating, and I started shaking. I needed to talk with someone. I used calling cards back then, but did not have one that night. I started calling my brother Adao (Adam in English) using my landline without the card. I didn't care what the cost was going to be. I wanted to hear his voice that night. I called him several times, but there was no answer. I kept walking impatiently around the basement apartment until the morning arrived.

Adao was the seventh child in the family—a beautiful, caring, compassionate, and fun soul. He was a handsome young man who attracted many girls in his high school. He was a fantastic brother to me and my siblings and a great son to my parents. He had such admiration and respect for my parents that no matter what time he arrived home, sometimes late at night, he would go and check on my parents to make sure they were well or just to let them know he was home. He always sang around the house and sometimes spoke through whistles, making everyone around him laugh. I cannot imagine anyone more organized than him. He kept everything in place, from his notebooks to his car. His car was always parked perfectly symmetrically into the spot so anyone who knew him would know he was the driver, even if he was driving someone else's car.

I was in my second year of college. Since Diolete (my oldest sister), Arlete (my younger sister), and Adao (my younger brother) were working in Mandirituba, we decided to rent a house that year so I could move from my friend Doroti's house. She had done enough, hosting me for a year in her home. Adao was attending a high school that year, evening classes. The bus station was about ten blocks from the house. As a caring young man and a lovely brother, Adao would go to the bus station every night and wait for me so I wouldn't walk by myself late at night when I returned from college. He was always in good spirits. We would walk laughing a lot about any silly thing we saw on the street or stories we told each other about what had happened that particular day. Everybody loved Adao. He was a young man with a great character and charisma that radiated love and laughter around him. I knew that one day, he would be a great husband and a fantastic father. I was seven years old when he was born, and as I close my eyes, I remember that March morning of 1978. He was a blond baby. My parents now had mixed kids from red to blond hair and all skin colors, which is the beauty of interracial culture. I would be a fool if I said he was not perfect because he was. There was always love, care, and laughter around him.

That morning, I didn't feel like going to work, but I had yet to miss a day in the United States, so I drank my coffee, put on my white outfit, and walked to the train station in Lyndhurst, New Jersey. People on the train seemed to be sad that morning. Maybe they all had a nightmare like I did. I sat in my usual seat on the third car of the train. I closed my eyes and could still see that scene of trucks on the highway.

I was still bothered by the dream, and since it was said that one of the bodies was my "friend," I emailed a friend of mine before I started working, telling him about my dream.

"Dear Mario, I had a nightmare last night about an accident. I was told that a friend of mine had died in the accident. I don't know what that means, but in any case, be careful today when you drive to work." I don't remember if he ever responded to that message, nor do

I know why I had chosen that particular friend. I have no idea what brought me to do that.

I had been working for Dr. Behnam. I had started at the front desk and had learned everything about the office. I was now the office manager. Through the years, I have met many cancer survivors and have been touched by their stories. I had also witnessed the pain that many families endured when the surgery, chemotherapy, and radiation therapy didn't work and the cancer took their loved ones. Years earlier, I had the opportunity to meet Jamie, a beautiful, lovely, charismatic young woman who survived ovarian cancer three times. Jamie had experienced pain too many times and lost all her hair. The cancer was coming and going, and she still kept a bright smile on her face. Every time Jamie came to the office, her presence spread love in the air. I always think of Jamie with love. She taught me resilience, perseverance, never giving up, and believing I could overcome adversity. As I write these lines, Jamie still teaches dancing classes in New York City.

Two days later, I was at work getting ready for the day. The patients were already in the waiting room when my cell phone rang. On the other line was my brother Adao's fiancée, Eunice. Eunice had a great sense of humor and never started a conversation without laughing, but that morning, she was crying, and what she was about to tell me would change my life.

"Hi, Janete. Adao died in an accident last night."

I could not believe what I was hearing. My brother Adao, dead? "No, no, and no. That's not true!" I shouted.

I could not ask anything else as the tears were coming, and every memory started playing like a movie in my head, repeating itself for what seemed forever. I had just lost part of me and could not get that part back. My heart was in pieces and pain. If I had only known that the last day I would have seen Adao was the day I was leaving for the United States, I would have hugged him more. I would have told him how much I loved him, if I had only known.

That morning, the patients in the office came around my desk and expressed their condolences. I didn't want to add my pain to theirs, but at that moment, it was inevitable. Dr. Kazem Behnam was such a great doctor—very calm and compassionate. He was used to seeing people in pain, and he understood mine. He hugged me and gave me some comforting words that he knew what I was going through, and my brother was now an angel in heaven.

My emotions were so high, and I could not think clearly or make any decisions. I don't know who called my friend Doris. All I know is that she was there to pick me up in a matter of minutes. She took me home, and little by little, I was trying to understand the tragedy that just had happened. My brother's dream was to be a truck driver. He was amazed at how big the trucks were and was fascinated with traveling cross-country in Brazil and getting to know different cities. My parents never liked the idea and tried to discourage him, but at the same time, they wanted him to do what made him happy. Finally, he got a job as a truck driver and was fulfilling his dream. He was happy with the job and had worked for the trucking company for about three months. My mother told me he had been home that morning and complained of a toothache. He didn't feel like traveling that night as the next day would be Corpus Christi. (Corpus Christi is a religious holiday in Brazil; generally, people don't work that day.) But he had to deliver the merchandise on time. He had no option but to go. Nobody knows for sure what happened that unfortunate night. My family was informed that the truck lost its brakes when he was driving down the mountain in Capao Alto in the State of Santa Catarina, South Brazil, and the lumber that he was transporting fell into the driver's side and made the truck flip, killing him instantly.

I couldn't stop crying. I cried for days. I was not able to eat or sleep. I was looking pale and frail. I was mad at the world and God and wanted to die. The clouds of sadness that had surrounded the truck drivers in my dream that night were now present in my life. My brother was twenty-seven. He was engaged and would get married in December (2005). He was madly in love with Eunice, his high school sweetheart. As one of the traditions in Brazil, his future in-laws gave them a piece of property where they had built their future home. He was ready to marry and start a family. Due to my immigration status at that time, I was not able to travel. My lawyer had advised me that if I left the country, I would not be able to enter the United States for ten years, and I would have to start the immigration process again. Even if I could travel, attending my brother's funeral in Brazil would have been impossible as his body would have been buried within twenty-four hours of his death. In my hometown and many regions of Brazil, it's common for people to hold wakes in their houses, unlike the elaborate funeral services often seen in the United States. I was experiencing the loss of my beloved brother and, at the same time, the feeling of not having the freedom of leaving and coming back. There was no one to blame but myself. I had decided to stay in the United States and had to deal with the consequences.

During the months following his death, I thought about going back home. I was alone in this country and felt lonely, but as difficult as it was, I sincerely believed that my American dream was just getting started. One night, I had a dream about my brother. He was in a beautiful place with bright and peaceful music in the background. He had this angelical and blissful face as he always did. He asked me to stop crying and never give up on my dream, as he had fulfilled his purpose on earth and was well and in a great place. He said he would understand every time I would cry if I missed him but asked me not to cry because he had died. He said my life would improve despite feeling lost, and our family needed me to stay in the United States. He certainly knew the family needs more than I did at that time. He then whistled with a happy sound. I then asked about the "friend" who had died and who he/she was. "We cannot see each other as we are in different places. There is a gate between us. It's better if you don't know this person's name." With that, the bright light was gone, but the music in the background continued playing while I was sleeping.

I remember my brother with love. I miss him daily, and I often recall the great times we spent together laughing about silly things. I keep his picture with his truck on my desk, and every day I look at him, I feel his approval that I didn't give up on my dream.

After living in America for several years, I feel more American than Brazilian. I still follow some of my family traditions and customs. One of them is visiting the tomb of a loved one who has passed away, so I decided to adopt a grave at the Lyndhurst Cemetery in New

Jersey. I often bring flowers to that grave and pray for that unknown soul. He might be that "friend" who died and needed my prayers.

The death of my brother Adao left a hole in my heart, and I was living in a shadow of sadness. My days had no color, only a mist of darkness surrounding me. During the day, I kept myself occupied at work and interacting with people, and their health concerns made me forget my problems. Still, when I got back home, I encountered pain and anguish again in my wounded heart—a severe and inexplicable discomfort mixed with emptiness and filled with anger in the silence of my apartment. Horrendous thoughts kept asking why it wasn't me instead. I have been far away from my family and it would be less painful for them if it were me who died. Those feelings were attached to me and refused to go away as I felt that part of me had died. I lost interest in the future. I lost the motivation to stay in America and was planning to return to Brazil against my counselor's advice. Alana, a friend from college, had been in the United States for three months and had helped me cope with my grieving, but she had left, I was alone and lonely. After I had that dream with my brother, I started putting my broken pieces together and gained the strength to decide to stay and start making a better version of myself.

The Twist

It was October 29, 2005, and it turned out to be a turning point in my story. I had been invited to a Halloween party at a friend of a friend's house, and I decided to bring my friend Anzor as my guest. Anzor and I had first met at Passaic Community College in Paterson, New Jersey, when we were taking advanced English classes, and had become close friends. He was a smart, outgoing, and hilarious Russian guy. Our get-togethers were always filled with laughter, and we were both excited about the upcoming party, especially since we had such a great time at a Halloween party the year before. However, life had a different plan in store for me that day.

I lived in a quaint basement apartment with an antiquated heating system. Interestingly, the primary heating system for the rest of the house was also situated in the basement. One day, my landlady, who was around the same age as me, encountered an issue with her heat and had to call the public service to come and fix it. As I returned home from work, I settled in and began chatting with a friend on my laptop. It was at this moment that the technician from PSE&G (Public Service Electric and Gas) made his entrance into my living space. I distinctly recall him wearing a sky-blue T-shirt, prompting me to think, *"Hello there, kind of cute; what are you doing here?"* Though I attempted to disregard this reaction, I couldn't help but steal glances in his direction as he went about his job.

The problem appeared to be more complex than the technician had initially anticipated. Consequently, he had to call in another technician to provide assistance. Meanwhile, my landlady descended on my apartment to talk with the technician, who formally introduced himself to me.

"Hi, I am Nick."

"Nice to meet you. I am Janete."

He asked my landlady if he could turn off the heat in the basement. She agreed but mentioned that I was Brazilian and always felt cold. The word "Brazilian" caught the technician's attention, and he began sharing his own love story involving a Brazilian woman. While he was talking, I couldn't help but wonder why we couldn't connect since we were both here and I was single. Despite these thoughts, I continued listening. After he finished his work and was leaving, I offered to help him and his "girlfriend" if she ever returned to the United States. I added, "Whenever she comes back, just stop by and bring a friend," to make it clear that I was single.

I was having a casual conversation with my landlady when I opened up about my fondness for Nick. After our friendly chat, she excused herself and went back to her apartment. Moments later, my phone began to ring, and I anticipated that it was Anzor calling to confirm our attendance at the party. To my surprise, the caller was Nick. He had actually contacted my landlady to inquire about my contact details and then took the initiative to invite me for dinner.

"When?" I asked. "Tonight," he replied.

I was completely confident that I would accept the invitation, but at that moment, I didn't feel like explaining my reasons, especially since I had already made arrangements for the Halloween party.

"Let me get back to you in a few," I said, and I hung up the phone.

I dialed Anzor's number, feeling a pang of guilt as the phone rang. When he answered, I hesitantly explained that I wouldn't be able to make it to the party. Concern seeped through his voice as he asked if everything was okay, but I could sense his unspoken question about whether I had a date instead. Despite his subdued reaction, I could tell he was disappointed. Sadly, that was the final exchange we had. I find myself longing for his vibrant personality and recalling the moments of joy and laughter we once shared.

THE DIRT ROAD

I was absolutely thrilled when I got the chance to confirm my dinner plans with Nick over a phone call. In anticipation of the evening, I carefully selected a stunning black tailored jumpsuit that accentuated my figure and paired it perfectly with a long, elegant white leather coat. With great attention to detail, I completed the ensemble with a pair of chic, stylish high heels that elongated my legs. After meticulously styling my long hair and applying my makeup to absolute perfection, I felt confident and ready for the occasion. As I sat waiting for the date, I couldn't help but feel excited for the evening ahead.

Nick treated me to a lavish evening at an upscale restaurant featuring live entertainment, creating an atmosphere reminiscent of a night at a Broadway show. Having experienced heartbreak and disappointment in the past, I had become disillusioned with relationships and had resigned myself to the belief that the possibility of finding a genuine connection was slim. I had convinced myself that independence was the path for me and that marriage was not in my future. I didn't anticipate anything exceptional from that evening, only potential future headaches. However, unexpectedly, I had an incredibly enjoyable time that night.

Nick claimed that he had to work overtime that day and after a long day, his boss asked him to do one more job. When he checked his computer queue, he found two addresses - one was mine and the other belonged to someone else. He hesitated for a moment and then decided to choose my address. After leaving my apartment, he got into his truck, updated the company's computer, and thought to himself, "*I like this girl. I am going to ask her out.*" He returned and knocked on my door, but I didn't hear it. Determined, he called my landlady and asked for my phone number and name; he couldn't remember my name for some reason.

The following day, I stuck to my routine and went to mass at Our Lady of Pompeii church in New York City, just like I had been doing for several years. When I returned, I arranged to meet Nick at a quaint coffee shop in Rutherford, New Jersey. That evening was truly memorable. We had a wonderful time discussing a range of topics, including my immigration status in the United States, the passing of my brother that year, and my aspirations to open my own business that winter. In addition, Nick shared captivating stories about his Italian family, his experiences at PSE&G, and his involvement in a bowling team.

After a month of dating, I was taken aback when Nick asked me to join him at his twenty-fifth high school reunion. As I agreed, I couldn't help but wonder if I needed to reassess my views on relationships, particularly with men, while remaining careful not to get hurt again. Upon arrival at the reunion, Nick introduced me to his best friend, Charlie, and to my surprise, Nick used the words "my girlfriend", signaling that our relationship was more serious than I had thought. As our bond deepened, it became clear that our relationship might or might not stand the test of time, but I felt prepared for whatever the future held, given my age and maturity.

Nick and I had been dating for over a year since I received the life-altering news about my immigration papers that Mrs. Behnam had filed years earlier. The devastating revelation was that my work permit had been denied, leaving me with a difficult choice. I had to decide whether to leave the country or stay and risk being considered an illegal resident. The decision weighed heavily on me as I had recently launched my own medical billing business, which was showing promising signs of success. The thought of starting over in Brazil, my home country, was daunting, especially considering the competitive job market and the fact that I would be perceived as too old to secure a good position. Despite my reservations, taking risks had been a recurring theme in my life, and I found myself at another crossroads. Additionally, I knew marrying a United States citizen would alter my immigration status within six months. However, I had always told Nick that I would only consider marriage for love.

On June 13, 2008, as we made our way along Route 17 South near Paramus, New Jersey, Nick asked me to spend the rest of my life with him in a heartfelt and unconventional proposal. In a sentimental touch, he used a plastic ring he had purchased as a joke during a previous trip to Florida, as the real ring he had ordered had not arrived in time. This impromptu proposal, lacking in traditional pomp and circumstance, was a genuine reflection of our love for each other. It was a moment that resonated deeply with me, and when the official ring did arrive, Nick asked me again, this time formally, to be his partner for life. Nick then planned a civil ceremony for July 31, 2008, ten months before our church wedding, a decision that held special significance as it was instrumental in securing my legal residency in the United States.

On May 2, 2009, at 3:15 p.m. in New York City, I walked down the aisle at Our Lady of Pompeii church. The Ave Maria by Schubert, sung by Eva P., filled the air. I wore a gorgeous wedding gown, had perfect hair and makeup, and felt like an angel. The church was beautifully decorated by my friend Fabio B. with the Brazilian tradition of my hometown, flowers lining the benches, and a white carpet. Fabio also created my stunning bouquet with exotic flowers. The Catholic ceremony was performed in Portuguese, Italian, and English, so our families from Brazil and Italy could understand when they watched the video. I chose to walk down the aisle by myself as I didn't want anyone to take my father's place. Sadly, none of my family members could attend due to visa issues. After the church ceremony, we had a wonderful reception at The Venetian in Garfield, New Jersey, where our 227 guests enjoyed hors d'oeuvres at the cocktail hour with the gentle sound of a harp, followed by a formal dinner as we celebrated our love story in grand style.

Two days after our beautiful wedding in the United States, Nick and I boarded a plane headed to Brazil to celebrate with my family on May 8, 2009. The ceremony took place at the stunning Nosso Senhor Bom Jesus church in my hometown, and it was a deeply emotional and meaningful experience. Walking down the aisle with my parents by my side was a moment I will cherish forever. My father, who had suffered a severe head concussion in a car accident years earlier, may not have fully comprehended the occasion, but his emotions spoke volumes. Little did I know at the time that it would be the last day Dad would walk. My oldest sister, Diolete, poured her heart into decorating the church, creating a truly enchanting atmosphere for the ceremony. The Wedding March filled the air as we made our way down the aisle, surrounded by the love and support of our family and friends. Despite already being married, the local priest generously allowed us to have a formal ceremony, creating a deeply meaningful and significant moment for us and my family. It was a moving and emotional occasion as Nick's family was unable to attend the ceremony. However, to uphold the Brazilian tradition where the mother of the groom escorts the son to the altar, I asked my dear friend Alana to accompany Nick in place of his mother. Alana, who speaks English, graciously stepped in adorned in a stunning red dress for the occasion. Throughout the ceremony, she stood by Nick's side, offering him unwavering support and love, representing the role of a mother for the ceremony.

As the ceremony ended, Nick and I walked out with a song declaring, "My parents will be your parents, and your parents will be my parents." This touching melody not only marked the end of our beautiful Brazilian wedding ceremony but also symbolized the deep bond forming between our families. My father's affection for Nick was evident, and my mother's adoration for him knew no bounds. I also formed a strong connection with Nick's parents. Mr. Francesco Parente and Mrs. Nevina Parente have embraced me as their own, and I cherish them dearly as if they were my own parents.

Following the church ceremony, we celebrated with a modest yet heartwarming reception, steeped in the overwhelming love and support of those closest to us.

During the reception, Nick suddenly asked me, "Who was that guy who walked towards the back of the room?"

"Who?" I asked.

"This guy came in holding a child's hand, looked at me, and walked to the back of the room. Then he came back, looked at me again, and walked out. I saw him and the child get into a truck, and then they left," Nick said.

I was confused and asked my siblings and friends if anyone had seen a stranger crash the party, but no one had seen anyone. My late brother Adao's fiancée happened to be seated where the "guy" had walked, but she did not see anyone who didn't belong at the party. My sisters and I were intrigued by this event, and we somehow wanted to know why Nick was the only one who saw the stranger. That was when Mom said, "That was your brother Adao. He came to meet Nick, and he is happy for you." If that was who it was and if possible, the child that Adao held hands with was my first brother, whom I had never met. Maybe it was an assurance of the dream I had with him, reassuring me that everything would be okay.

Going Back Home

"Welcome to Aeroporto Internacional Afonso Pena, Curitiba, Brazil," said the pilot. I looked out the window, and it was surreal. I couldn't hold back my tears any longer. My palms were sweating, and my heart was racing in my chest. My legs trembled as my husband and I wheeled our suitcases to the exit. The doors opened, and I saw Mom and my brother Jair with open arms waiting for us.

So much remained unsaid as I embraced my mother and brother, and tears of joy cascaded down, forming a river of happiness.

As my new husband and I exited the BR-116 highway, we turned onto the dirt road to visit my family. Due to the lack of rain that fall season in my hometown, the car stirred up dust as we drove. The gray clouds moved slowly and silently across the sky, and the only sound we heard was our breathing. I marveled at the road, which was unchanged during my absence, a path I had walked so many times before.

It had been a whole ten years since I last set eyes on my family. During that time, I had missed numerous significant events - from weddings and birthdays to funerals. I can still vividly recall the image of my younger sister, Dine, who was nine years old when I left. She was an adorable little girl with the most mesmerizing smile. Her soccer skills were remarkable, and I can still picture how she effortlessly kept the ball bouncing on her foot for an extended period. As for my youngest brother, Jackson, he was only seven when I bid them farewell. A cute little boy who was a die-hard fan of his soccer team, Gremio, would only wear his black, white, and blue jersey from his team. I have the fondest memories of how he would impatiently wait for his favorite shirt to dry, often walking around the house shirtless until it did. Now, as I await our reunion, I can't help but wonder about the changes that have taken place in their lives over the years.

The deep lines on my parents' faces told a unique story. Years passed, and they held memories of strength, obstacles overcome, wisdom, and love. It had been ten years since I had seen them last. As I hugged them, I felt their hearts beating in contentment that their child was back home.

All my family was gathered, waiting for our arrival. Tears of joy flowed down everyone's faces as we exited the car. Everything looked different; we all had aged, but love remained unchanged. It was as if I had never left.

I glanced at the kitchen table, and the polenta I used to dislike, which has now become my favorite dish, was on the table with chicken, tomatoes, and onion salad, just waiting for me. We laughed!

On September 21, Brazil celebrates Arbor Day. Its main objective is to raise environmental awareness, and the day was chosen because of the beginning of spring, which starts on September 23 in Brazil. Everyone is encouraged to plant a tree that day. When I was in school, we either planted a tree around the school or received a plant to take home. I was rarely enthusiastic about the plants I was given because I was always planting them around the farm, and there were so many naturally occurring plants there that I couldn't get excited about a new one. But when I was ten years old, I received an ipê plant to take home, and I was intrigued by it because there were no ipê trees around the farm. So, I planted it, cared for it, and proudly told my siblings, "It's my ipê tree." It grew beautifully on the side of our house. It had been ten years since I had seen my ipê tree. The breeze touched the leaves and a unique smell wafted up; the leaves seemed to be dancing in contentment. I looked at it and realized how much I had missed those beautiful yellow flowers during spring, and even though it was not spring now, I could picture them and smell the unique sweet mixture of honey and strawberry in the air.

As I walked up to the house, I spotted my father's truck, a white and blue Chevrolet, parked on the side. I couldn't help but feel a sense of pride as I reflected on what that truck meant to my father and our family. Nick, who was with me, was visibly impressed by the old Chevrolet and even joked about buying it from my father. Intrigued, I took the opportunity to ask my father about Nick's inquiry, which sparked a conversation about the truck's history and sentimental value.

I asked, "Dad, Nick wants to know if you would like to sell the old Chevrolet."

"This old Chevrolet helped me provide for my family, and I will never sell it." He responded emotionally.

I was eager to walk around the house, checking things that I had missed. I started at my Mom's chicken coop. She had all kinds of chickens that looked warm and happy inside their abode. I was looking forward to hearing the rooster singing early in the morning. He once annoyed me, but I now wanted to hear it. I just needed to wait a couple of hours for that sound.

Sure enough, the following day, the rooster started with his melancholic crowing sound, and my husband, unfamiliar with such sound, could not sleep. I loved it and recalled all those mornings I had to get up. Now, I didn't have to, and his singing put me back to sleep again.

My brothers Joao and Jair had married, and I was officially introduced to their wives as their sister-in-law for the first time. I had known them before I left Brazil, and having them as part of my family was lovely.

My brother Jose Luiz was dating Dani, who had a son named Rafael from a previous marriage. Rafael, a very energetic kid with beautiful blue eyes and blond hair, instantly bonded with me. It was as if he was my own. Rafael brought my family a lot of joy, especially my mom. His arrival in our family helped heal my mom's broken heart after she had lost one of her own. It's amazing how God works in miraculous ways.

My brother Juarez was dating a beautiful girl. My sister Arlete was also dating a very handsome guy, and my sister Diolete was still single. I had all my siblings around me, and we started chatting about my life in America, how much we missed each other, and the events

I had missed. More than any activities, I missed my brother Adao. He had been gone for four years already. I choked, and tears tumbled down my face. I bowed my head and whispered, "You are not here. You are gone. I miss you."

The next day, my parents' house was full of visitors. Cousins, aunts, uncles, and old friends all came to see us, and they all had one question in common: "Is it true that in America, you only eat canned foods?" My husband was shocked when I translated such questions. He thought people would know more about America, but nobody knew anything besides canned food. He was disappointed but promised that with any opportunity he had, he would show them what America is all about—the beauty, the food, the culture, the history, etc. And he did and still does every time we travel to Brazil. "Where do these people get that from?" he asked. "From the movies," I said. Then my husband got his iPhone and showed them pictures of the best supermarkets in America with various fruits, vegetables, meat, etc. Every year, when we go to Brazil, we encounter people who ask us the same question. It became a joke between us. Every time we buy canned food, we shout in the kitchen, "Don't let Brazilian people know we are eating canned food."

The Promise

"I, Janete Teixeira, take you, Nicolas, for my husband to have and to hold from this day forward for better, for worse, for richer, for poorer, in sickness and in health until death does us part. I will love and honor you all the days of my life." Those were traditional and beautiful wedding vows that I pronounced at my wedding according to my Catholic faith.

Nick and I had been married for two years. We were committed to working hard, saving money, and buying a house of our own. Finally, we found a small house in the town we wanted to live in. We were very excited to start the process of buying it and becoming homeowners. It wasn't the perfect house we had in mind, but it was in a great neighborhood, had a wonderful property, and, above all, it was what we could afford.

It was my fortieth birthday, and I wanted to celebrate with my family and friends in Brazil. I made all the arrangements for my party and traveled there. Even though I've been in the United States for many years and have made amazing friends here, my old friends are still in Brazil. I feel fortunate to still have an incredible group of friends from high school. We used to gather to celebrate our birthdays during high school, and I wanted to continue that tradition for my fortieth. I cherish every opportunity to be with them. True friends are always there for you when you need them most—whether you need a shoulder to cry on, someone to celebrate your achievements, or even someone to hold you accountable when necessary.

I have a very special memory of my birthday celebration in America, thanks to my dear friend Geni. We first met at a language school while I was learning English, and our friendship has been a blessing ever since. On my birthday, feeling a bit lonely, Geni surprised me with the most delicious homemade cake. She invited me to her cozy house, where she had prepared a beautiful celebration just for me. With a warm smile, she sang "Happy Birthday" to me, and in that moment, I felt an overwhelming sense of love and belonging. It's a memory that I hold dear and will always cherish.

I had an amazing time celebrating my birthday with my friends and family, but now it was time to return home and deal with the house. A lot of work needed to be done before we could move in. Nick had changed his work schedule to help our contractor during the day. He would go to work at 3:30 p.m. and return home around 12:15 a.m. After several weeks, he started complaining about his lack of sleep and feeling the urge to cry. I encouraged him to let it out, but he said he couldn't. One day, he left early to help the contractor at our new home. Something didn't feel right that morning, so I left everything I was doing and went to check on him. When I arrived at the house, I found Nick sitting on the front steps, looking lost and in agony. He couldn't express himself, and I was scared, but I tried not to show it. I wanted to take him home, but he insisted on finishing whatever he had started that morning. Later, when he returned home from work at midnight, he couldn't hold back the tears. I watched as my strong husband collapsed in tears with horrific chest pain. I called 911, and in a matter of minutes, the ambulance arrived and took him to the hospital. After being evaluated by the ER doctor, he was diagnosed with a panic attack that led to severe depression.

I had made a promise to Nick, vowing to stand by him in sickness and in health. Now, I find myself living out those very words. Mental health disorders are truly challenging to comprehend unless you've experienced them firsthand or witnessed a loved one struggle. Despite no issues in our marriage or financial hardships, my husband was facing a tough battle. We led a comfortable life with a home, money, food, and cars, but my husband couldn't even care for himself. While I had a business to run and meetings to attend, my top priority was to shield my husband from the torment that consumed his mind. I understood that depression could lead to dark thoughts, so I was petrified to leave him alone at home, so I never did. I brought him everywhere, and he would wait for me in the car. Nick is talkative and opinionated on every subject, but those rides were silent. Despite the overwhelming fear and uncertainty that washed over me, I summoned all of my courage and determination to hold my position as a wife and a friend to my husband. The once resilient man I married was now fragile, tormented, and in constant sadness. He had lost interest in everything, and his physical appearance was sometimes barely recognizable.

The mainstay of treatment for depression is usually medication, talk therapy, or a combination of the two. To normalize the brain changes associated with depression, it's imperative to find the right medication, but in Nick's case, we couldn't find the right one. While running to the doctor's office with him, I trusted my faith in God, and together with my family and friends in Brazil, we were praying that we would find the right medication.

It's very sad to know that some people are nonchalant regarding mental health. I experienced firsthand my husband being judged as a weak man when he was terrified and imprisoned inside the inescapable swamp of his depression.

At times, I felt utterly helpless because I couldn't find answers, but I did know depression was a serious illness, and not for even a second did I make any judgment about my husband's condition. I was by his side as a wife, friend, and, above all, a good listener. Sometimes, I was just there sitting by his side without saying a word, and that was what was needed.

My parents taught my siblings and me to care for each other, be there, and support each other no matter what. My younger sister Dine had been my father's caregiver, so she understood the stress I was experiencing. I would text her in the middle of the night to share my anguish, despair, and fear. She would comfort me and assure me that everything would be okay. More than ever, I wished my family was here, especially my three sisters, but there were thousands of miles between us.

There were days that I needed emotional support and felt that I was going to fail at any given moment, but I needed to be strong for my husband. Years earlier, on several occasions, I had seen my mom stand by my father's side for reasons that were not necessarily sickness, and Mom would say, "I married your father for good and for worse." Mom's example of love, faith, and compassion gave me strength to endure the difficult times I experienced in my married life.

After several weeks, the right medication was found, and little by little, with the help of talk therapy, my husband felt better, and we started getting back to our normal lives. This chapter of our marriage has made us grow strong. We held it together when life tested our courage, strength, faith, and love. We didn't quit.

My Mother

It is often said that determination is a driving force that enables us to cross paths with individuals from diverse backgrounds, each playing a significant role in reshaping our lives. Without a shadow of a doubt, my mother stands out as the most influential figure in my life. Her remarkable strength and resilience have left an indelible mark, fostering a deep sense of confidence and unyielding enthusiasm as I navigate the challenging road to success.

My mother has faced many hardships and challenges throughout her life, but she has always shown incredible resilience and strength, which is why I greatly admire her. She experienced a series of unfortunate events, including the loss of my elder brother shortly after his birth, dealing with an alcoholic husband for many years, and the loss of another child when he was 27. She had eleven pregnancies, most proceeding without any health issues, except for the eleventh one. When my youngest brother was on the way, she was already forty, and due to her advanced maternal age, she faced complications such as high blood pressure, weakness, and glucose imbalances. Her health declined rapidly, and she had to be hospitalized around her thirty-fourth week of pregnancy. I remember visiting her in the hospital and thinking that she might not survive. She was so ill that she couldn't even speak. It was horrifying to see her in such a state, especially when she was still working on the farm just a few months earlier, taking care of the house, kids, and chickens. Despite her condition, she remained faithful and whispered to me that she was certain God would save her and her child. After a month in the hospital, she underwent an emergency C-section, and my youngest brother, Jackson, was born healthy and beautiful.

Mom has made enormous sacrifices throughout her life to ensure the happiness of her children. One unforgettable moment occurred during my high school years. I had a psychology assignment on one of Sigmund Freud's theories, and the teacher requested that we find a baby to bring to class. Fortunately, my younger sister, Dine, was three months old then, and I asked my mother if she could bring Dine to class for the assignment. Without hesitation, my mother walked five kilometers on the dirt road from our farm to my high school to help me with the project. At the time, I failed to grasp the depth of my mother's love and dedication, but looking back, I am profoundly grateful for her incredible act of kindness and love.

Mom has endured the adversities in life without fear. She had many reasons to be bitter, and yet I only saw Mom crying when she lost a loved one. I have promised myself to become as strong and positive as my mother and believe that events in life happen for a reason. When adversities happen, she says, "Don't worry. God knows what he is doing, and that's not for you." That saying didn't mean much as a young person, but as I grew older, it made much sense.

I had been married for over two years, and despite my hopes, I had not conceived. Unlike my mother, who had eleven children, I found myself struggling with the possibility of pregnancy. When I married at the age of thirty-eight, I was fully aware of the impact age can have on fertility, especially given my work in the medical industry. While I have nothing against single parents, I understood the biological challenges I might face as an older woman trying to conceive.

Initially we thought that it might not happen for us, considering our age. However, after a heartfelt discussion, my husband and I decided to pursue fertility treatments and explore all available options, in line with our values and financial situation. We wanted to ensure that we wouldn't look back and regret not having tried everything possible.

Going through fertility treatment was an incredibly emotional journey, with emotional pain greater than the physical. Over the course of three years, I sought the expertise of top doctors in New Jersey and New York. While some were incredibly compassionate, others treated me more like a statistic, yet all provided excellent medical care. Throughout this time, I underwent three intrauterine inseminations (IUIs) and eight in vitro fertilizations (IVFs). The experience of opening a box of medication, filled with pills and injections, measuring twenty-by-twenty inches, was overwhelming. Each new treatment cycle meant embarking on a daunting regimen of medications. The injections left my belly discolored, marked with shades of purple, red, blue, and gray. At a certain point, my skin had been so punctured there was no space left for another needle. Despite the immense pain, I knew it was necessary and I agreed to endure it. Over the course of three years, I received around five hundred injections in my abdomen, with the hope that each one would bring me closer to my goal.

In the early hours of the morning and late at night, my husband would assist me with my injections. However, due to his work schedule not always aligning with my medication schedule, there were times when I had to rush to Dr. Mel's house to have my injections administered. Dr. Mel was always generous with her time, helping me whenever needed. The side effects of the medication often caused bloating, giving me the appearance of being pregnant, even though that was merely wishful thinking. I'm aware that many women endure extensive challenges in their journey to conceive, with some undergoing more than eight IVF treatments. I deeply empathize with them and comprehend the emotional turmoil they experience.

Despite being well-informed about the statistics for women my age, I held onto hope that I would defy the odds and become the success story in this difficult journey. After the disappointment of the IUI not working, we turned our hopes to the IVF treatment, known for its intensity and higher chances of success. Following the setback of the first IVF attempt, my husband and I were reassured by our plan for three additional treatments with doctors in New Jersey. Each time we received a call from the doctor with a result, it was a crushing blow, yet we clung to the hope of another opportunity. However, when we received the news of the last result, it was a devastating blow, and our world shattered, and we were left questioning, "Why us?" Or rather, "Why not us?"

In our pursuit of parenthood, my husband and I sought a new doctor in New Jersey to help us. During our initial consultation, the doctor thoroughly reviewed my medical records and discovered that I had uterine fibroids. She recommended that we address this issue before moving forward with any fertility treatments. I agreed to the doctor's plan and underwent an open surgical procedure to remove the eighteen fibroids attached to my uterus. It was a challenging process, but I focused on my recovery and healing.

Once I had healed from the surgery, I eagerly resumed my visits to the doctor to begin a new fertility cycle. The fertility facility in New Jersey had an excellent success rate for women in my age group, which gave us renewed hope and optimism. I diligently followed the prescribed medications and injections, as well as undergoing regular ultrasounds and early morning blood tests. The doctor closely monitored my progress and was pleased with the results.

I vividly recall the excitement we felt during the ultrasound monitoring sessions when the doctor would report the growth of the eggs, saying, "One, two, three, four eggs growing. Looks great." I was overjoyed when the doctor informed us that six good eggs had been retrieved during the egg retrieval procedure. Our excitement soared even further when, upon our return for the embryo transfer, we learned that I had four good-quality embryos. It was a moment filled with immense sentiment and expectation as we dared to hope for a positive outcome in our journey toward parenthood.

My dear sister-in-law Dani and I grew closer during that challenging and emotional period. She is a woman of profound faith who has weathered tragic events with grace and resilience. Despite everything, she never wavered in her trust in God. Dani would wake up in the dead of night to offer heartfelt prayers for me and Nick. She recorded those prayers and sent them to me, asking God to comfort our hearts if having a child was not part of His plan for us and to safeguard the medical professionals and caregivers looking after us. Waking up in the middle of the night to listen to her prayers, I felt as though God was right beside me, holding my hand.

I had become accustomed to waiting, but this time, I could barely contain my excitement for my pregnancy test. The day began with joy in the air, but my doctor's phone call shattered it all - the procedure had failed again. Tears flowed as the doctor discussed alternative options that contradicted our beliefs. Despite feeling like it wasn't meant to be, I couldn't shake the feeling that there was more to try.

We sought a new, exceptional doctor in New York City, but my age posed a significant challenge again. I embarked on four more cycles of IVF, feeling more hopeful than ever when the first cycle yielded twenty-two eggs - a remarkable feat given my age. However, this achievement meant nothing if the embryos couldn't survive in my uterus, which they never did. I faced disappointment after disappointment, each IVF negative result taking a greater toll on me emotionally. I was devastated and hopeless when I received the last call from the doctor's office with my very last IVF results, and I had to come to terms with the fact that our dream of parenthood would not be attainable. Despite this, we accepted that we had done everything possible and had no regrets.

During a challenging and emotional time, I was shown a beautiful gesture of love and compassion by three remarkable women: my friends Carla Loaiza, Sandra Jory, and my sister Dine. Sandra and Carla, both mothers, generously offered to carry embryos for me if my uterus was the issue for conception, but it turned out not to be the case. The thought of these incredible women enduring a full-term pregnancy for both me and a child who wouldn't be biologically theirs is truly touching and represents unconditional love. The doctor explained that it was not my uterus's age but the egg's that was the issue. I am incredibly grateful for such a selfless gesture, and there are no sufficient words to express my gratitude.

Despite our distance, my sister Dine's unequivocal support during the entire process meant a lot to me. When I mentioned the age factor affecting the eggs, she selflessly offered hers without a second thought, saying, "I can give you mine. I am younger than you." Her words moved me to tears, her love and selflessness shining through. Despite our decision not to pursue her offer, the depth of her care and support will always stay with me.

In the weeks following my last treatment, I continued to grapple with the outcome. It took several therapy sessions with a medical professional for me to come to terms with the fact that I would not become a mother. However, a conversation with my mother provided the most comfort. She revealed that she had been praying for me throughout the treatments, asking for a sign from God about whether having a child would truly bring happiness into my life. She expressed her desire for a miracle while also praying for an outcome that wouldn't subject me to the same pain she experienced from losing two of her own children.

My life is filled with people who can be considered heroes in various ways, but none can compare to my mother. She has always been my guiding light and my source of strength. I hold an immeasurable amount of love for her in my heart.

COVID-19

I was drinking my morning coffee and looking out the kitchen window, watching the beauty of the tall and graceful oak trees in my backyard. The once-green-and-vibrant grass had been decorated with yellowish and golden-brown heart-shaped leaves gently falling, waving, and dancing in the wind as they dispatched the last stages of life before tumbling to the ground. There was a chill in the air; to me, it seemed the leaves were declaring that something was coming other than winter. I don't think I had ever appreciated their beauty like I did that October morning.

The day would have been normal if it wasn't for the noise on TV with headlines of lockdowns, masks, and social distancing. The days had already seemed unreal, like the world was in a total mess, all of humanity surprised by the pandemic's acute respiratory illness caused by a virus. COVID-19 was capable of producing severe symptoms and death, especially in those with underlying health conditions.

Something did not feel right that morning. I fixed my eyes on my father's picture attached to my refrigerator door. We had lived about five thousand miles apart for twenty-one years. I have been married to a United States citizen and lived in suburban Fairfield, New Jersey, while my dad was still living in the same small rural community of Agua Clara in Brazil, where I was born. That morning, I felt his presence in my kitchen, as if he was having coffee with me. Suddenly, a beautiful golden-brown, yellowish leaf hit the window and caught my eye. I looked again at my father's photo. Was my father trying to tell me something, or was I just missing him? I often miss my father, but that morning, it was a mix of sadness and grace that I never experienced before. I closed my eyes, and in a matter of seconds, I felt that an angel had taken me to a cloud full of colorful light and then brought me back to my kitchen.

My phone rang, and I heard my youngest sister on the other end. Dine's eyes sparkle with joy, which usually came through in her voice too. But that day, she had a saddened, slow, and anxious voice.

"What happened?" I asked.

"We are taking Dad to the hospital. A doctor and a nurse are here. We all are being tested for COVID-19."

I immediately made a video call. I wanted to see my dad, and more than anything, I wanted to hear his voice.

"Hi, Dad, how are you doing?"

"I am well," Dad responded. "Are you and Nick okay?"

It was springtime in Brazil, a sunny, beautiful day. My mom, my dad, my youngest sister Dine, and my oldest sister, Diolete, were all outside on the patio with the doctor and the nurse as they tested for the virus. I noticed that the flowers on the ipê tree on the side of the house were shining like the sun. Even in that short conversation, I could feel the warmth through my father's eyes, an expression of love and the confidence that he had radiated, stronger than ever. He looked directly at me and said, "God bless you." It's been a tradition in my family for generations to ask our parents for a blessing instead of any other greetings, and in return, their answer is always, "God bless you." My ancestors believed that one couldn't thrive in life without the parents' blessing.

I didn't want to think that could be our last conversation, but I realized that if it was, I could be sure that my father loved me and was proud of the person I had become.

My father was a strong man, and I don't remember ever hearing my father complaining about pain. Whenever my sister Dine posted a picture of him on our family group on WhatsApp, I was the first to comment on how handsome our old man looked. That day wasn't any different. I thought he looked the same as I had seen on our last video call two days earlier, and his voice and face seemed the same. I could not understand why they were taking him to the hospital, so I asked to speak with the doctor.

The doctor answered my questions in a very calm voice, "He is coughing, nothing serious. We are taking him to the hospital just to run some tests, and hopefully, he will be back home soon."

"Do you think my dad has the virus?"

"I can't tell you that, but we'll have the results at the hospital in a few hours. If he is infected, we will transfer him to the Hospital of Rocio in the City of Campo Largo, a better hospital. As you probably know, our local facility cannot care for coronavirus patients well."

I did know how deprived the health system is and how it works in Brazil, especially in small cities like Mandirituba. Following the end of the military dictatorship (1964–1985), the 1988 Constitution established "health as a fundamental right and a responsibility of the state," with provisions to create a unified national health system, the Sistema Unico de Saude (SUS). This was reinforced by the principles of equality, solidarity, and social participation intended to develop a universal, comprehensive, and decentralized health system free of charge for its citizens. However, the free-of-charge healthcare system in small cities tends to be inadequate, with precarious equipment and, in some cases, with no medicine or medical providers available to treat patients with severe medical conditions. Unfortunately, the system threatens the health of its citizens, as only those who can financially afford to have a doctor outside the SUS can survive in some cases.

It's about 3.1 miles along a dirt road from my dad's farm to the nearest hospital in the small city of Mandirituba, and then from there to the Campo Largo hospital is a trip of about 36.6 miles.

"Doctor," I pleaded, "can you please take good care of my dad?"

For hours afterward, I kept imagining I heard the loud siren of an ambulance in my ears. That afternoon, I was informed that my dad had tested positive for COVID-19 and he was already transferred to the Hospital of Rocio in Campo Largo. Although my father had been in a car accident years ago, had his right leg amputated, and had been bedridden for many years, he did not have any of the worrisome underlying conditions such as diabetes or hypertension. Despite the accident, he was a seventy-nine-year-old who took only one single medication to sleep. Part of me was confident that my dad would be back in his own home soon, but the other part was already preparing for loss.

The virus would pick off the weak from the strong. My sister Dine, my mother, my brother Juarez, and my brother-in-law, Rafa, all tested positive for COVID-19.

My world was collapsing. Fifty-three years earlier, my parents had vowed to be together in good and bad times, in sickness and health, and they truly lived what they promised each other. Mom had a fall when she was eight months pregnant with her first child, and due to a lack of medical providers around the farm, the baby was born premature and only survived a month. They were a young couple starting a family with so much sadness about losing a child, but God blessed them with ten more. They faced enormous difficulties raising ten children in a small house with no electricity, running water, and little money, but they did. Years later, she lost another child at the age of twenty-seven in a tragic accident. They were again heartbroken, but their vital companionship, love, and faith kept them strong together. My siblings and I had been loved unconditionally by my parents. They taught us through their actions of respect, sacrifice, grace, honesty, and dignity, which have created waves of love for our future generations. My mother had all the worrisome underlying conditions, including diabetes, hypertension, and poor blood circulation. She took at least eight different medications daily. I was already mentally exhausted, overwhelmed, and with so little time to process my emotions. I broke down in tears, frightened that I was going to lose my family.

The pandemic had been devastating in Brazil. Even with the country's state governors imposing lockdowns, use of masks, and quarantine to prevent the spread of the virus; in October 2020, there were approximately 150,000 deaths, second-highest death total after the United States.

The transformation couldn't have been crueler. Within twenty-four hours, the infected's fever spiked, and they were coughing. My mom was ill, pale, and frail. The virus was not only on TV; the invisible enemy was attacking my family. As the days passed, Mom started getting better, but my dad's condition was declining. The hospital informed my family that he had been intubated and his lungs were 80 percent compromised. Only a miracle could save his life.

Though separated by 4,868 miles, my family and I prayed together. Meanwhile, I had a profound and honest conversation with God. I didn't ask God not to let my father die. Instead, I asked him not to let my dad suffer anymore. There had been enough suffering throughout his life. Besides the car accident that stole the use of his legs, he had suffered the loss of his first child, endured the difficult life on the farm raising ten children, and lived through two eye accidents, almost losing his vision, plus the death of another child at age twenty-seven. I asked God to forgive Dad if he had hurt anyone or left an unhealed wound in anyone's heart. "Please, God, give my dad a peaceful ending."

I momentarily thought about jumping on a plane. Though there was a traveling ban between Brazil and the United States due to COVID-19, having dual citizenship, I would be allowed to enter and leave Brazil anytime. But what difference would that make if no one was allowed into the hospital? My family and I trusted that the hospital's updates every other day were accurate. Together with my siblings, we decided that I would remain in New Jersey and continue to be together in prayers and trust the will of God.

God will do what's best for Daddy, we agreed.

After fourteen long days in agony. I still had a business, deadlines, and clients to answer to. I was not able to concentrate on anything. Nothing was making sense to me. My nights were sleepless, and I was looking pale. My husband was concerned that the exhaustion, stress, and lack of sleep were going to make me ill.

An early voice message on WhatsApp from my brother Jair on October 21, 2020, would change everything: "Daddy has left us, and it is with a heart full of sorrow that I will be doing the body recognition in a few minutes."

Jair didn't know the routine procedures for identifying a departed loved one or understand that the pandemic had turned normal upside down.

Minutes later, Jair sent a new message: "The doctor told me that Daddy is in a body bag already, and I have to trust the hospital and just sign the papers. The hospital is following their local health authorities' guidelines for COVID-19, and the funeral home will take the body directly to the cemetery."

That was awful to hear, and there were no words to express my feelings. The thought that my father was in a bag. In a bag? The scene I had seen on TV—the trucks in New York City waiting for the COVID-19 dead bodies—started playing in my mind, and now my father was in a bag!

I know, of course, that death is inevitable and beyond anyone's control. It does not choose color, race, ethnicity, or religion, but it is a universal process that will eventually occur in all human beings and organisms on earth. No one knows the day or time. Death arrives when you least expect it and abruptly takes those you love the most.

My siblings and I called each other for a brief conversation. Our voices were suffocated by grieving tears and disbelief that Dad was truly gone. It was tough to manage our emotions, and we started questioning. How about if it's not our dad? We all wanted to find something, some person, or event to blame. Who could we blame? China? Lockdowns? Travel ban? Why did he have to die from this virus? How about if the hospital made a mistake? But then suddenly, there was a pause, and the reality sank in: Daddy had left the earth. Our dad was dead, and we could not do anything other than grieve the loss.

Just as technology played an essential role for medical providers during the pandemic, it also allowed me and my husband to view Dad's funeral through a video call. We watched his sealed casket, decorated with a yellowish garland of flowers, arrive at the cemetery as my immediate family gathered in prayers for the last goodbye.

As the casket was slowly lowered into the tomb, my six-year-old niece, Iara, in tears and inconsolable, walked by the casket and said, "Goodbye, Grandpa. I will always love you. I will miss you." She then placed a white flower on the top of the casket, and slowly, quietly, like a leaf falling from the tree, the grave was closed.

There is a season for everything.

The Angel at the American Consulate

In 2015, my sisters Diolete and Dine applied for their visas to visit us. Unfortunately, their applications were denied without any explanation, leaving them extremely disappointed with the process.

In 2018, my sister Dine and my mother both applied for visas, hoping to visit the United States, but to our disappointment, their applications were denied once again. It was particularly perplexing and disheartening when my elderly mother's visa was denied. At the time, she was in her late sixties and posed no threat. I found myself grappling with the question: Did the authorities perceive her as a potential threat to the United States or perhaps as someone who could take away job opportunities from locals? This situation left me feeling deeply irritated, prompting me to express my frustrations by emailing the White House. Despite my understanding that a response was highly unlikely, I felt compelled to voice my concerns nonetheless.

In 2019, I enlisted the services of the very attorney who had previously guided me through the green card application process. Her team diligently completed the necessary steps and submitted an application for my mother's visa. I meticulously ensured that all relevant documents, including the farm property deeds, my father's medical records, and my mother's retirement payment statements, were professionally translated from Portuguese to English by an accredited

THE DIRT ROAD

translation company. Despite the thorough preparation, the approval of my mother's visa remained uncertain.

My siblings and I decided that only our mother would apply for the visa. My sister Dine was quite anxious about this because Mom would have to go to the interview all by herself, as they didn't allow anyone to accompany the applicant. We were concerned that during the interview, she might be asked a question and then struggle to remember the answer.

The day before the interview, my sister Dine and Mom embarked on a flight to Porto Alegre, the stunning capital of Rio Grande do Sul, the southernmost state in Brazil that shares its borders with Uruguay and Argentina. Dine confided in me that on the eve of the interview, she offered a heartfelt prayer, pleading with God to send an angel to guide Mom through the upcoming interview. Upon their arrival at the American consulate, they were met by a man dressed in a pristine white uniform, who warmly greeted my sister with the words, "Don't worry. I will help your mom." With a reassuring touch, he placed his right hand on my mother's shoulder and led her into the interview room while my sister looked on. Her prayer had been answered, and joyful tears came down her face. After what seemed like an eternity, my mother returned with a radiant smile gracing her face. "My visa was granted," she exclaimed joyfully as she enveloped my sister in a warm embrace.

The COVID-19 pandemic took the United States by storm, causing significant stress and uncertainty throughout the nation. As a business owner, I had to quickly adjust to the new circumstances by transitioning my employees to remote work and devising strategies to ensure the continuity of our operations. Just a month before the lockdown in the United States in 2020, I had traveled to Brazil to bring my mom to visit; she now had her visa and would be able to legally enter the United States. Upon returning to the United States, I vividly recall watching the news as Brazil reported its first case of COVID-19. "It was a significant moment, as the pandemic emerged in São Paulo on February 26, 2020, when a sixty-one-year-old man developed severe acute respiratory syndrome after returning from Turin, Italy", the headline said.

My husband and I were overjoyed to welcome my mom into our home. After twenty-one years of living in America, having my mom as the first member of my family to visit us was truly special. Her presence during such challenging times was a comforting and cherished blessing. We cherished our time together, bonding over cooking, having delightful conversations over coffee, indulging in Brazilian soap operas, and sharing hearty laughter. To me, it felt like fate had a hand in it all. Due to the lockdowns in both countries, my mom's return home had to be postponed, and what was meant to be a 30-day visit turned into 120 days. When she finally got her chance to fly back, her connecting flight was canceled in Brazil. My brother, Jair, went above and beyond, driving five hours to São Paulo to pick her up and bring her home.

During the challenging time of the lockdown, I truly believe that I wouldn't have been able to cope with the overwhelming stress without my mom's love and support. I found myself struggling with many challenges and feeling isolated and abandoned. It felt as if, for a brief period, people had overlooked their empathy and become absorbed in their own needs and financial concerns. Despite sharing the uncertainty brought by COVID-19, the bond of understanding had frayed.

The weight of uncertainty bore down heavily on me – the future of my business and the welfare of my clients hung in the balance. My primary worry was for my employees, each with their own families to support; the mere thought of letting anyone go was unbearable. Drawing from my own past experiences, I've always been able to empathize with others. Yet, at the end of each challenging day, I found relief in the support of my mother. In moments of despair, I became a child again, finding comfort in her embrace and the love and understanding that only a mother can provide. In those moments, her gentle, reassuring words echoed in my mind, "Everything will be okay."

My top priority was to protect my mom from contracting the illness that was spreading rapidly. For 120 days straight from February to June 2020, my mom and I decided to remain indoors, proactively taking measures to safeguard our health and well-being.

Throughout that time, I was constantly vigilant in ensuring that my mom was shielded from the potential risks posed by the virus, and I was firm in my efforts to keep her safe.

I cherished those moments I spent with my mom. As we reminisced about the past, we shared laughter and tears. Her recounting the angel at the American Consulate evoked powerful emotions we struggled to contain.

Family and Family Roots

Where did we come from? This question of my origins had long perplexed me. I strongly desired to uncover the intricate tapestry of my family history. While aware of our Portuguese heritage on my father's side, I remained in the dark about the specifics and the number of generations. As for my mother's lineage, my knowledge was scant, hinting at a possible Japanese heritage. My husband and I eventually decided to undergo a DNA test, revealing my roots as Portuguese, Native Indian, and with traces of Asian ancestry. However, these revelations only pique my curiosity further, compelling me to seek a deeper understanding of our family's past.

During a memorable trip to Brazil, I decided to delve into my family history by undertaking a genealogical search. To aid me in this exploration, I contracted the services of a specialized company from my hometown. Their research discovered fascinating details about my family's origins through a comprehensive review of various historical documents.

My father's ancestors came from Portugal to Brazil in 1500. Our family roots trace back to Jewish-Sephardic heritage, with ancestors who were Jews living on the Iberian Peninsula in Portugal and Spain. In 1492, King Ferdinand and Queen Isabella of Spain expelled all Jews who refused to convert to Christianity. Many fled to Morocco, Portugal, Turkey, and beyond, while those who stayed had to conceal their Jewish identity. The introduction of the Inquisition in Portugal in 1536 led to waves of Jewish emigration. The pressure to escape persecution from Portugal was also driven by the search for economic opportunities in countries like Brazil. I have traced my roots to names such as Antonio Rodrigues de Alvarenga (1550–1614), who was married to Anna Ribeiro (1559–1647), and Antônio Bicudo Carneiro (1540–1610), who was married to Isabel Rodrigues. They were Sephardic Jews and part of the founding families of important cities like Curitiba, the capital of my state of Parana. I am the sixteenth generation of my family.

In 2015, Portugal enacted a law that allowed individuals of Jewish Sephardic descent to apply for citizenship if they could provide appropriate documentation, regardless of the number of generations that had passed since their ancestors lived in Portugal. However, in August 2022, amendments were made to the law, requiring applicants to prove their descent and demonstrate links to Portugal. Having learned about this before the law was changed, my siblings decided to apply for Portuguese citizenship. While I opted not to apply due to already having dual citizenship, I am excited about the positive opportunities this will bring to my siblings.

As for my Native Indian and Asian roots, I am still searching.

The importance of family in our lives cannot be denied. In my opinion, family is the critical root of anyone's journey. The feeling of unhappiness I once had towards my mom for having more babies has nothing to do with the person I have become. In fact, I now wish my mom had had more children. The child who once despised farm work now profoundly admires and respects the dedication and hard work of farmers who ensure that we all have food on the table.

Returning home once or twice a year is truly incredible. The warm reception and love that my husband and I receive fill our hearts with joy. My husband and I are greeted by the loving embrace of my mother, the joyful presence of my siblings, the delightful energy of my nieces and nephews, and the kind welcome of my brothers and sisters-in-law. Despite the language barrier between my husband and my family, we gather in the cozy living room, exchanging stories and sharing heartfelt laughter until I get tired of being their translator in both Portuguese and English. In these cherished moments, there's no place I'd rather be than surrounded by the love of my family.

I often think about my eldest brother, whom I never had the chance to meet. I wonder what he would have been like, the things he would have enjoyed, and the person he would have become. Every single day, I long for the presence of my dear brother Adao. Despite the ache in my heart, I take comfort in the belief that he now resides in heaven, bringing a sense of peace to my soul.

My siblings and I have a group chat on WhatsApp with Mom, and we make it a point to communicate daily. Sometimes, it's just a simple good morning or good night, but it's our way of showing love and care for each other. Sharing our life events with each other makes me feel connected as if I'm just around the corner.

I am deeply thankful for the strong family values my parents instilled. Their support and guidance have given us the skills and optimism to face the world. Their unconditional love, faith, and encouragement to express ourselves respectfully while considering others' needs have played a crucial role in shaping who we are today. My family home embodies safety and warmth - a place where my siblings and I gather, share laughter and embrace each other.

Living far away from home has allowed me to appreciate and cherish my family even more. Despite our imperfections, we have grown to embrace our unique qualities, offering a hand in times of need and always being present for one another.

I am incredibly thankful to have the Behnams as my family in the United States of America. Their love and acceptance from the moment I stepped into their home have profoundly impacted me. Initially, my acquaintance was limited to Dr. Behnam and Mrs. Behnam, but later, I got to know Bob, Ross, and Melody. Over time, Bob earned the title of Dr. Amir Behnam, Melody became Dr. Melody Behnam, and Ross embarked on a career in law. Despite feeling like a stranger in their home, I was consistently treated with kindness and respect and never once felt diminished due to my immigrant status, even while performing household tasks. Although homesickness often plagued me, each time I walked through their doors and saw one of them, it felt like reuniting with one of my siblings, and it always brought a sense of peace to my heart. Many times, seated at their beautifully set table, surrounded by the comforting warmth of a loving family, I found immense joy in sharing a meal that had been lovingly prepared by Mrs. Behnam for all of us. The taste of the food and the heartfelt conversations intermingled to create a profound sense of belonging and gratitude in those deeply cherished moments.

The love, support, assistance, and compassion that the Behnams have shown me has been woven into the very fabric of my being. The memories of their friendship, love, and care are etched deep within my heart and soul, creating a sacred space I will forever cherish. Their selfless acts of kindness have left a permanent mark on me. I am passionately dedicated to perpetuating their legacy of generosity by paying it forward and spreading their goodwill to others in need.

My two families have been crucial in shaping my personality from the dirt road to America.

My Two Nations

Whenever I hear the Brazilian anthem, I am moved to tears, and I can't help but join in singing when I'm in a place where the national anthem is being played. Brazil will always hold a special place in my heart. Every time I set foot in Brazil I recite the nostalgic lines of "Canção do Exílio" that I first learned as a child. I have a deep affection for my culture: the mouthwatering food, the vibrant music, and the passion for soccer. However, in my heart, there is no place like America, the land of the free and the home of the brave.

America, with its vibrant cities, each with its unique character and cultural offerings—from the busy streets of New York City to the artistic flair of San Francisco and the historic charm of Philadelphia, Boston, and Washington, DC—there is something for everyone to explore, enjoy, and be proud of.

America, a place that I thought would be my home for a while, is now my country. I am proud of my adopted country and appreciate the principles of freedom, democracy, and equality upon which the nation was founded.

I am profoundly thankful for the incredible opportunity that America has provided me. This great nation not only opened its arms to welcome me but also presented me with the chance to shape a brighter future for myself and my family. The kindness, support, and unity I have experienced from my fellow Americans have left an indelible mark on my heart. Colleagues, friends, clients, and even strangers have extended their warmth and assistance, enabling me to pursue my aspirations and transform my visions into reality in this amazing land of boundless opportunities.

America is a fascinating country. It's not perfect, as no nation is, but it is the best place to live. There are opportunities for everyone, regardless of race, nationality, or beliefs, and it's up to each individual to take action, work hard, and make the American dream a reality. Along with these opportunities comes the responsibility of being a good citizen, respecting the laws, and contributing to a better society.

> One man can make a difference, and every man should try. (John F. Kennedy)

While working on the farm in Brazil, I envisioned a better life, and America helped me turn that vision into a reality.

Thank you, America.

Acknowledgements

I acknowledge my deep gratitude for God's constant protection, guidance, and light in my life. Especially during the years dedicated to this writing project, my faith has been my rock, and without it, I could not have persevered to see it through.

My husband Nick has enriched my story in so many ways. You have been a great help when I encountered difficulty translating some stories from Portuguese into English, and you have added insightful comments that led me to write a better story. Thank you for being part of my story and for loving me unconditionally.

I am incredibly grateful to Lisa Romeo, my first writing coach, for your invaluable direction and instruction in helping me assemble my initial stories when I felt completely lost about how and where to begin. My heartfelt thanks go out to you.

I will forever be thankful to Lacey C. Clark for providing me with all the necessary tools and guidance to compile my story. It wasn't just about teaching me; you truly believed in my capabilities! The moments we shared during our morning Zoom sessions for the writing project were truly priceless, and they will always hold a special place in my heart. Your support and mentorship have been truly phenomenal!

This book would not have been possible without the incredible Jennifer Altmann. I am extremely grateful to you; not only did you teach me, but you also enthusiastically believed that my story deserved to be shared with the world. Your guidance and suggestions have been incredibly valuable to me. Thank you!

I want to express my gratitude to the incredibly talented cover designer Nina Ovryn for her amazing skill in transforming a simple iPhone picture into a breathtaking work of art.

I'm really grateful for the contribution of my dear friend and talented photographer, Keila Botsolas, who used her skills to capture my photo for this book.

My dearest sister Edinete Alessandra (Dine), I am truly grateful for your kindness in taking all the pictures I requested from the dirt road. Your thoughtful gesture means the world to me. I want you to know how much I value and appreciate everything you do. I love you beyond words.

I am eternally grateful to Professor Antonio Lourenco dos Santos for his significant contributions to the history of Mandirituba. Your teachings and wisdom shaped my worldview, and your impact continues to resonate profoundly within me.

I want to express my gratitude to Mr. Dionizo Gelenski for generously sharing details from his personal story with me, which is included in this book. Since I was fourteen years old, Mr. Gelenski and his family have warmly welcomed me into their lives, treating me as one of their own. I am profoundly thankful to be part of their incredible family and to have the Gelenski family play a significant role in my life story.

Kristie Wright from Christian Faith Publishing, with every phone call you made, you left me with a word of encouragement, which has made a difference. Thanks for believing in my project.

I would like to express my heartfelt appreciation to my dear friend Laura Hammer for her unwavering support and encouragement throughout the writing process of my book. She has been a constant source of motivation and inspiration, and I am truly grateful for her willingness to contribute by writing the foreword to my book. Her friendship is incredibly meaningful to me, and I am deeply thankful for her invaluable presence in my life.

I am grateful to my clients for being an integral part of my journey and for generously sharing their knowledge, warmth, and trust. Together, we have explored numerous paths over the years, and I sincerely appreciate your support. Thank you!

THE DIRT ROAD

I want to express my gratitude to Dr. Luke Eyerman for playing a significant role in the success of my business in America. I am forever indebted to you.

Last but certainly not least, I feel compelled to express my deepest appreciation towards my two families. Firstly, I want to extend my gratitude to my American family, Dr. Kazem Behnam, Mrs. Shahin Behnam, Dr. Melody Behnam, Dr. Amir Behnam, and Rostin Behnam. When I was twenty-nine years old, you embraced me, opening both your hearts and your doors, and giving me an extraordinary opportunity. You believed in me, and as a result, I was able to achieve great things. I feel incredibly fortunate to have all of you as part of my life story, particularly Mrs. Behnam, who not only became my adopted mother but also a remarkable mentor. You have been there for both my tears and laughter and have been a reliable shoulder to lean on at any time. I cannot adequately express how much love and gratitude I have for you.

My biological Brazilian family, my beloved and admirable mother Filomena (Filo), embodies faith, courage, love, and patience. Gratitude fills my heart for the gift of life and for the life of my dear siblings. Thank you for those cherished moments we spent delving into the rich tapestry of our family history that evoked both laughter and tears, weaving an indelible connection to our past. Your irreplaceable presence has left an enduring impression on the narrative of my journey. To Diolete, Arlete, Joao, Jair, Jose, Juarez, Edinete, and Jackson, my extraordinary siblings, thank you for crossing the rough and smooth paths of life alongside me.

My dearest father, Joao, your departure from this world came too soon. Not a day goes by that I don't miss you. I find comfort in knowing that you are now in heaven, free from the physical limitations you once faced on earth. I can feel your pride in me just as strongly as on my graduation day. You always encouraged me to pursue education, and I want you to know that I've written a book, Dad.

Although I never had the chance to meet my brother, Antonio Marcos, I often feel his angelic presence watching over me from heaven. It's comforting to believe that he is protecting me every day, and sometimes I feel like he is nearby, soaring like an angel.

My beloved brother Adao Joel, your passing has left a deep void in my heart. I think of you every day, but I take comfort in knowing that you are at peace. As I worked on this writing project, there were moments when I doubted myself, but in the stillness of the night, with just me, the computer, and your picture in my office, I felt your presence. I gazed at your photo many times, and in the quiet, I could almost hear you encouraging me with a whistle, saying, "You can do it." And I did.

About the Author

Janete Teixeira-Parente was born in South Brazil. She received her bachelor's degree from Pontificia Universidade Catolica do Paraná in *Secretariado Executivo*, she also earned an MBA from Universidade Positivo in Curitiba, Brazil. She is a business owner in New Jersey. The Dirt Road is her first book.

Printed in the USA
CPSIA information can be obtained
at www.ICGtesting.com
CBHW020200301124
18173CB00042B/402